CRANMER'S GODLY ORDER

The Destruction of Catholicism
through Liturgical Change

Part One of

LITURGICAL REVOLUTION

by

MICHAEL DAVIES

ARLINGTON HOUSE·PUBLISHERS
NEW ROCHELLE, NEW YORK

ACKNOWLEDGEMENTS

We are indebted to David and Charles for permission to quote from *Devon* by W. G. Hoskins in Chapters XIV and XV, to Basil Blackwell & Mott for permission to use material from *Eucharistic Sacrifice and the Reformation* by Francis Clark, and to Professor James Hitchcock for permission to quote from his book *The Recovery of the Sacred*.

ILLUSTRATIONS

BOOKS BY MICHAEL DAVIES

Liturgical Revolution:
Volume One: *Cranmer's Godly Order*

Liturgical Revolution:
Volume Two: *Pope John's Council*

Liturgical Revolution:
Volume Three: *Pope Paul's New Mass* (forthcoming)

Newman Against the Liberals
Selected and edited by Michael Davies

Originally published in Great Britain by
Augustine Publishing Co., Devon.

Library of Congress Cataloging in Publication Data

Davies, Michael.
  Cranmer's godly order.

  (His Liturgical revolution ; v. 1)
  1. Liturgics—History. 2. Catholic Church.
Liturgy and ritual—England—History. 3. Church of
England. Liturgy and ritual—History. 4. Cranmer,
Thomas, Abp. of Canterbury, 1489-1556. I. Title.
II. Series.
BV193.G7D38 1976   264'.03   77-4266
ISBN 0-87000-395-X (v. 1)

CONTENTS

CONTENTS

CONTENTS

AUTHOR'S INTRODUCTION

The Church is at present undergoing what is certainly the greatest crisis since the Protestant Reformation, quite possibly the greatest since the Arian heresy. Pope Paul himself speaks of the self-destruction of the Church and of the smoke of Satan having entered the Church. Priests and nuns are abandoning their vocations by the thousand; the number of vocations continues to decline; Mass attendance is plunging throughout the Western world; the most outlandish beliefs are put forward as Catholic teaching; the Church no longer makes any appreciable impact on society, as the dwindling conversion figures make clear.

This is also a time of convergence. The major Christian bodies are coming closer together in what they profess to believe and in their liturgical practice— talk of impending organic unity is ever more frequent. It is claimed that the work of evangelisation is greatly hampered by disunity among Christians, but it cannot be denied that the closer the separated bodies come together the less effective their work of evangelisation becomes and the greater the pace of their own decline.

This is also a time of confusion, particularly among Catholics. There is hardly a traditional belief or a traditional practice which has not been questioned or reversed. Priests who for decades had been telling their people why the Mass must always be in Latin now appear to believe that any of their parishioners who ask for a Latin Mass may be of dubious orthodoxy. Priests who for decades had been explaining why we could never take part in non-Catholic services now insist that taking part in such services is the prime duty of a Catholic. Not only that, but our own services are coming to resemble those of Protestants more closely, with each successive stage of the liturgical reform. A biography entitled *Pope Paul VI,* published by the Catholic Truth Society, remarks that the new liturgy has " close parallels with the Free Churches of England, Scotland and North America and Lutheran services ". Even extreme evangelical sects state that they have no objection to their members assisting at Mass and receiving Communion, as they see their own concept of the Lord's Supper in the new Catholic forms.

This liturgical convergence has been accompanied by doctrinal agreement. A joint Anglican-Roman Catholic International Commission has produced Agreed Statements on the Eucharist and the Ministry. Most people would agree with Bishop Alan Clark, Catholic Co-Chairman of this Commission, when he stated in his introduction to the *Agreement on the Eucharist*: " No one, only a few years back, could have believed that it would be seriously asserted that there is substantial agreement between Anglicans and Roman Catholics today as regards our faith in the Eucharist."

The manner in which these agreements have been reached is simple. The Catholic members of the Commission have allowed those aspects of the Catholic faith which the Protestant Reformers rejected to be either passed over in silence or worded ambiguously enough to make them acceptable to Protestants. This is made clear in a commentary by J. W. Charley, an Anglican member of the Commission, who points out that the *Agreement on the Doctrine of the Ministry* nowhere asserts that the Apostles appointed bishops and established an unbroken chain down to the twentieth century; that an ordained man is empowered to do anything a layman cannot do ; that a priest has the power to remit sins ; or that the Mass is a sacrifice. Another Anglican, the Venerable Bernard Pawley, Archdeacon of Canterbury, has praised the manner in which this " remarkable development " has been bolstered by an " unbelievable convergence " in the liturgical practices of the two communions.

It is obvious that in a period of militant secularism the restoration of Christian unity is an end for which we should all work and pray. But Christ came into the world to bear witness to the truth ; any agreement, any unity, which is not based upon the truth is not built upon Christ and consequently will not bear good fruit.

Bishop Clark remarks, in his introduction to the *Agreement on the Eucharist,* that: ". . . it would be wrong to expect to find in the Agreed Statement we are discussing the familiar terminology of Trent or the Anglican Articles. The whole purpose of this statement is to express the understanding of the Eucharist that underlies these formulae, to express the present faith of both Churches, and to do so in a language which people can understand today." The question to be decided is whether these Agreements really do express the understanding of the Eucharist which underlies these formulae. One of the reasons for which this book has been written is to make it quite clear that they do not. It will be shown beyond any possible doubt that the Eucharistic teaching of the Protestant Reformers cannot possibly be reconciled with that of the Catholic Church. If any Agreement is to be reached it must be by one of the parties concerned conceding that it has been mistaken. Mr. Charley certainly detects signs of this happening on the Catholic side in the commentary which has already been cited: " Faced with this range of agreed material, one is compelled to ask one searching question. Is there not here a change of theological stance on the part of Roman Catholicism? If ' change ' is too strong a word, then at least there appears to be a considerable shift of emphasis when these documents are compared with previous official statements."

Even more important than the question of these agreements on doctrine is the matter of the changes in the Mass. An examination of the new Catholic Mass makes it clear that the old Mass has been changed in a way which comes very close to what Cranmer did, and for which he has been censured by Popes, theologians, and Catholic historians. How can changes which have been regarded as reprehensible for centuries suddenly become admirable?

An equally important question is the manner in which these changes have come about. The obvious and accurate answer is—as a result of Vatican II. But how could this Council have resulted in such a startling breach with Catholic tradition and practice? Was the upheaval ordered or even desired by the Council? Must anything coming in the name of Vatican II be accepted uncritically?

In order to help remove some of the present confusion three key topics will be examined, God willing, in three separate books. The present, the first of the three, deals only with the Protestant Reformation. It explains what happened and why it happened. The second will deal with the Second Vatican Council, and the third with the liturgical changes which have followed that Council. The true significance of all these changes, which are still in process of elaboration today, and of their close inter-relationship, can only be appreciated properly within the context of the Second Vatican Council and in the light of the unprecedented innovations which inaugurated the whole process of liturgical revolution at the Protestant Reformation.

Unfortunately, the standard histories of the Reformation by such Catholic historians as Gasquet, Bishop, Hughes, and Messenger are now out of print, although they can be obtained from public libraries, as can the original writings of the Reformers, printed by the Parker Society. Happily, what is probably the fullest and most scholarly treatment of the theological impact of the Reformation in relation to the Eucharist is still available. This is Francis Clark's *Eucharistic Sacrifice and the Reformation.* The present work has the very modest intention of arousing interest in the Eucharistic controversies of the Reformation, controversies which have never been more relevant than at the present time of liturgical and doctrinal convergence. It is my great hope that many of those who read it will be sufficiently interested to go on to Francis Clark's authoritative work where most of the topics referred to here are dealt with at very great length and with very great scholarship.

In order to appreciate the significance of the liturgical changes made by the Reformers it is necessary to have a clear grasp of Catholic teaching on the relevant doctrines—particularly those of Grace and Justification. In their turn, these doctrines can only be appreciated within the context of the doctrine of the Mystical Body and the Incarnation. A chapter has also been included on Catholic Eucharistic teaching. The chapters on liturgical reform and the reform undertaken by St. Pius V will be found relevant not only to the changes made by the Protestant Reformers but to the examination of the liturgical changes following Vatican II which will appear in the third book of this series.

I would like to offer my sincere thanks to the theologians and historians who examined the typescript and whose criticisms resulted in the removal of its more serious deficiencies, the clarification of some obscure passages, and the addition of new and valuable material. It would be surprising indeed if some errors of fact or interpretation did not remain and any comments or criticisms of the book will be received with gratitude.

I would like to offer my very special thanks to Miss Kathleen Baker for typing both the draft and the final typescript and for her most constructive criticisms which have resulted in some important improvements; to Miss Bernadette Keenan for the beautiful frontispiece design which expresses what this book is intended to convey more effectively than anything that I have written; and finally, to Father Harry Marchosky who has been instrumental in more ways than one for both the writing and the publication of this book.

Michael Davies.

DEDICATION

To Father Oswald Baker,
Defender of the Faith

Ecce civitas Sancti facta est deserta.
Sion deserta facta est:
Jerusalem desolata est,
domus sanctificationis tuae
et gloriae tuae
ubi laudaverunt te patres nostri.

Rorate, caeli.

See how the Holy City is deserted now.
Sion is empty,
Jerusalem has been desolated,
The place where you dwelt
in holiness and glory
where our fathers
sang your praises.

Chapter I

ET INCARNATUS EST

CARDINAL NEWMAN has written that if asked to select one doctrine as the basis of our Faith: ". . . I should myself call the Incarnation the central aspect of Christianity, out of which the three main aspects of its teaching take their rise, the sacramental, the hierarchical, and the ascetic."[1]

God the Son united His divine with our human nature so that, as a beautiful Offertory prayer expresses it, "we may be made partakers of His divinity." Catholic theology lays great stress on the fact that the Incarnation was made dependent upon the co-operation of Our Lady. The Sin of Adam had turned man against God and lost us the right to heaven. Mary's "Fiat" set in motion the train of events which would reverse this situation. Through this "Fiat" Our Lord Jesus Christ entered this lowly world, explains Pope St. Leo: "coming down from His heavenly throne yet not leaving His Father's glory, born in a new order of being, by a new birth. He was born in a new order because, invisible in His own essence, He made Himself visible to us; incomprehensible, He willed to be comprehended; subsisting before time existed He began to be in time; Lord of all things, He took on the form of a servant, dimming the glory of His majesty; God impervious to suffering, He did not disdain to become a man who could suffer, and immortal though He was, to submit to the laws of death."[2]

Everything connected with the Incarnation is a mystery, as Dom Guéranger makes clear. "The word of God Whose generation 'is before the day star' is born in time—a child is God—a Virgin becomes a

Mother and remains a Virgin—things divine are commingled with those that are human—and the sublime, the ineffable antithesis, expressed by the Beloved Disciple in those words of his gospel, ET VERBUM CARO FACTUM EST, is repeated in a thousand different ways in all the prayers of the Church ;—and rightly, for it admirably embodies the whole of the portent, which unites in one Person the nature of Man and the nature of God."[3]

The Christian religion is founded upon the reality of the Incarnation as an historical fact.   Remove that reality and nothing remains, as Cardinal Newman makes clear: " The Incarnation is the antecedent of the doctrine of Mediation, and the archetype both of the Sacramental principle and of the merits of the Saints.   From the doctrine of Mediation follows the Atonement, the Mass, the merits of Martyrs and Saints, their invocation and *cultus*.   From the Sacramental Principle come the Sacraments properly so called ;   the unity of the Church, and the Holy See as its type and centre ;   the authority of Councils ;   the sanctity of rites ;   the veneration of holy places, shrines, images, vessels, furniture and vestments . . . You must accept the whole or reject the whole ;   attenuation does but enfeeble, and amputation mutilate."[4]

The Christian religion stands or falls upon the historical fact that at a given moment in time the Word of God took to Himself our humanity, our poverty, our nothingness, to give us in exchange the power to be made sons of God.   This is teaching upon which both Catholic and Protestant would be in accord, presuming neither had succumbed to the Modernism infecting both communions, a Modernism which has the reality of the Incarnation as its principal target, having correctly assessed that it is the cornerstone of the entire fabric of Christian doctrine, whether Catholic or Protestant. Where non-Modernist Catholics and Protestants would disagree is on the emphasis to be placed on the role of Mary in the Incarnation—but on the historical reality of the Incarnation and its role as the foundation of our religion they would be in accord.

CRUCIFIXUS ETIAM PRO NOBIS

Just as non-Modernist Catholics and Protestants agree on the reality and the importance of the Incarnation they would also agree that the Incarnate Word redeemed mankind by offering His life upon the Cross of Calvary. Sin is a culpable rejection of the grace which God offers gratuitously to man. It is more than an offence, it is a perversion of nature for it is intrinsically unnatural for the creature to reject the Creator's will. The meaning of Redemption can be traced back to two Hebrew roots which signify the buying back of a loved one from slavery.[5] All mankind has stood and stands in need of redemption, both as a result of original sin and of the guilt incurred by each individual when he accepted the godlessness of his fallen state by personal sin. Western theology holds that Jesus Christ has made super-abundant satisfaction for sinners by dying for all. St. Thomas teaches that: "He properly atones for an offence who offers something which the offended one loves equally or even more than the detested offence. But by suffering out of love and obedience Christ gave more to God than was required to compensate for the offence of the whole human race."[6] Scripture and all Christian tradition consider that the Passion of Christ is the one atoning sacrifice by which the world is saved.

"But God shows His love for us
in that while we were yet sinners
Christ died for us.
Since, therefore, we are now justified by His blood,
much more, now that we are reconciled,
shall we be saved by His life . . .
As one man's trespass
led to condemnation for all men,
so one man's act of righteousness
leads to acquittal and life for all men." (Romans V)

Gabriel Biel who died in 1495 has been termed the last of the medieval doctors. He was the most widely read authority on the Mass at the time of the Reformation and summarised the accepted Christian teaching on the atonement in one of his sermons: "Here we are considering the whole manner of our redemption. When, long ago, Our Lord offered up His passion He redeemed the whole human race once and for all from the wickedness of the devil ; He opened the locked gates of heaven with the key of His Cross ; by pouring forth His blood He cleansed all things."[7]

There is a difference of opinion between Protestant and Catholic theology not in the fact that Christ atoned for our sins once and for all upon the Cross but in precisely how He did so. The Church has not finally pronounced upon this matter and it has long been a matter for speculation among the different schools of theology within the Church.[8] The principal difference between Catholics and Protestants, particularly at the time of the Reformation, lay in the portrayal by the Reformers of Christ's Passion as a substitutionary punishment demanded by divine vindicatory justice. "This is the most terrible thing of all," wrote Luther, "that Christ was smitten and put to the torture by God, and so took upon Himself God's anger . . . for nothing else could have placated the anger of God but a sacrifice so great as this—the Son of God."[9] Francis Clark explains that if Christ's sacrifice was *essentially* a penal substitution which had averted God's anger from the elect to Himself, then it was *past*. There could only be a thankful memory of such a sacrifice. ". . . the Church could not by a sacramental rite perpetuate its reality nor mediate its efficacy to men."[10]

Catholic theology, based on St. Anselm, explains Christ's sacrifice as vicarious satisfaction freely offered by Our Lord, making amends by His personal dignity for offence given by His fellow men to divine honour.

The moral value of an act before God derives not only from the content of the act but from the dignity of the agent. In this case, the agent being Jesus Christ, both God and Man, the dignity of the act is infinite and divine, and therefore more than able to compensate for the glory of which God had been deprived through sin. The acceptance of Christ's sacrifice by God as satisfaction for the offence of sin, a fact made clear in numerous

scripture references, means that He has redeemed us by
offering infinite satisfaction for the sins of the world as
the representative of humanity.[11]

It was not the physical suffering and death of Christ
which was pleasing to God but the *love and obedience*
which inspired His Passion. This was well summarised
by St. Bernard when he wrote: "Non mors sed
voluntas placuit sponte morientis."[12]

Although Christ's passion was sufficient in itself to
atone for the sins of the world and redeem all men it
does not follow that all men will be redeemed. A
distinction must be made between the *sufficiency* and
efficacy of His great act of atonement. The fruits of the
Passion are available to all but they will be efficacious
only in the case of those who freely co-operate with
divine grace to achieve their personal salvation. This
will be dealt with in more detail in Chapter II.
Explaining the question of sufficiency and efficacy in
relation to the consecration of the wine during Mass,
the *Catechism of the Council of Trent* states: "if we
look to its value, we must confess that the Redeemer
shed His blood for the salvation of all ; but if we look
to the fruit which mankind have received from it, we
shall easily find that it pertains not unto all, but to
many of the human race (non ad omnes, sed ad multos)."
The Catechism explains that for this reason the form
for the consecration of the wine uses the words "pro
multis"—for many. "With reason, therefore, were the
words 'for all' (pro universis) not used, as in this place
the fruits of the Passion alone are spoken of, and to the
elect only did His Passion bring the fruit of salvation."[13]

MYSTICI CORPORIS CHRISTI

Through the Incarnation of God the Son, men became
His brethren according to the flesh and were able to
regain their lost inheritance when, by means of His
great redemptive act upon the Cross, He not only
placated the outraged justice of the Father but merited
an immense treasury of graces for mankind. It was

stated above that Catholic and Protestant alike are agreed that the merits of Christ's Passion were sufficient to redeem all men once and for all. It is on the question of *how* these merits were to be applied to men that a radical difference of opinion arose between the Reformers and the Catholic Church. It is this question which lies at the basis of the Reformation and it is vital to realise that the Reformation was essentially a dispute concerning doctrine. Those who study the writings of the Reformers will find that it is questions of belief rather than questions of conduct which concern them. There is no question as to the fact that the Church was in need of reform in the sixteenth century, as it has been so many times during its history—the concern of some of the most saintly Popes, such as Gregory the Great, has been to bring the members of Christ's Mystical Body to practise a manner of living which conformed in the closest possible manner to the pattern set by and required by their Head.[14]

But although the Reformers attacked the abuses which existed within the Church this was done mainly from a propaganda standpoint: their principal attack, the raison d'être for their *new* religion, was their refusal to accept fundamental Catholic teaching.

God can bestow the merits won by Christ directly upon individual men without the use of any intermediary, but His plan is that these merits should normally be distributed by means of His visible Church, a Mystical Body in which Christ is the Head and the Holy Ghost the soul, giving the human members the grace required to *co-operate* with their Head in His redemptive work. God has chosen to redeem us by the means of the Incarnation which required the co-operation of Mary's "Fiat." He could have redeemed us in some other way which would not have required human co-operation—but it was His will that He should redeem us by means of the Incarnation. Reflecting upon the Incarnation makes it easier to understand what Pius XII explains as one of the most perplexing aspects of the mystery of the Church. Pope Pius writes that it is certain, surprising though it may seem, " that

Christ *requires* His members." He makes it clear that
Christ requires this help not by necessity but by choice
(just as He chose to become incarnate with the co-
operation of Mary). ". . . our Saviour wants to be
helped by the members of His Mystical Body in carrying
out the work of Redemption. This is not due to any
need or insufficiency in Him, but rather because He
has so ordained it for the greater honour of His
immaculate Bride. Dying on the Cross, He bestowed
upon His Church the boundless treasure of the Redemption without any co-operation on her part ; but in
the distribution of that treasure He not only shares this
work of sanctification with His spotless Bride, but wills
it to arise in a certain manner out of Her labour."[15]

The Catholic conception of the Christian religion can
aptly be described as " incarnational."[16] Christ's means
of applying the merits of His Passion is to continue the
Incarnation throughout time until He comes again. He
does this *not* simply through the effects of the Incarnation but by prolonging the Incarnation Itself—and this
prolongation of the Incarnation *is* the Church, Christ's
Mystical Body which is Christ Himself living and acting
through His members who transform the world by the
divine life of Grace which flows to the Church through
Christ Her Head. Christ has communicated not only
His holiness and merits but His powers of sanctification
to His hierarchical Church. " Endowed with Christ's
priesthood, the Church through Her ministers has the
function of *mediating* to all men the fruits of Christ's
all-sufficient work of salvation. This is the ' work,' the
opus operatum of the sacramental system."[17] It is this
concept of the Church and Her priests *mediating* between God and man, dispensing the Grace won on the
Cross by means of the Sacraments, which evoked the
wrath of the Protestant heresiarchs. It is therefore
important that Catholics have a clear understanding of
the concept of the *opus operatum*. This is explained in
Appendix I.

P. Bertrand excud

The Crucifixion: *plate from a 1652 French edition of the*
Missale Romanum

Chapter II

THE CATHOLIC DOCTRINE OF JUSTIFICATION

" Ex inimico amicus "

THE KEY to the Reformers' breach with traditional Catholic teaching is found in their doctrine of Justification by Faith Alone. Its logical consequence was the rejection of the Church and the whole Catholic sacramental concept. Their hatred for the Mass cannot be appreciated adequately without some understanding of their teaching on Justification, but before doing this it is necessary to clarify what the Church teaches. In a brief study of this kind it is not possible to study the Catholic teaching in any depth and such complex matters as efficacious grace and predestination will not be touched upon.

Justification involves the establishing of a right relationship between God and man in the light of the Fall, of making man just in the sight of God. In Catholic theology this is achieved by man's acquisition of a new life with new powers and new privileges ; a participation in the divine nature by the indwelling of the Blessed Trinity. This will culminate in the beatific vision, the sharing in God's knowledge and love of Himself, by union (though not identity) with the Son, the Word of God. The new life bestowed upon the justified man is the life of grace, and wherever grace is mentioned in this chapter it will refer to sanctifying grace unless actual grace is specifically mentioned.

The great benefit of Justification is, as Cardinal Newman explained, " This one thing—the transference of the soul from the kingdom of darkness to the kingdom of Christ."[1] It is, to quote the Council of Trent, " not

only the remission of sins, but the sanctification and
renovation of the interior man through the voluntary
reception of grace and gifts, whereby a man becomes just
instead of unjust and a friend instead of an enemy (ex
inimico amicus), that he may be an heir in the hope of
life everlasting (Titus 3 : 7)."[2]

CHRIST THE CAUSE OF GRACE

Trent teaches that while the final cause (the ultimate
purpose of and reason for) justification is the glory of
God, " the meritorious cause is the beloved and only-
begotten Son of God, our Lord Jesus Christ, Who when
we were enemies (Rom. 5 : 10), by reason of His very
great love wherewith He has loved us (Eph. 2 : 4),
merited justification for us by His own most holy
Passion on the wood of the Cross, and made satisfaction
for us to God the Father."[3]

Christ our Lord is the cause of grace and the first
and greatest gift of grace. He is our Emmanuel, " God
with us "; forgiveness and redemption are the gifts He
bestows upon us.

Grace is our adoption as sons of God, not adoption
in the normal legal sense but actually a rebirth. A
human parent who adopts a child can give it only his
name and the rights of sonship ; he cannot beget it
again so that it becomes a child of his own blood, shares
his nature as it were. Through grace we are begotten
anew and actually share in the divine life of God ; our
nature is " divinised " by sharing in the divine nature.
We are, as the beautiful Offertory prayer expresses it,
" made partakers of His divinity Who vouchsafed to
become partaker of our humanity." Through grace we
are able to " put on " the Son of God and become " heirs
of God and fellow heirs with Christ " (Rom. 8 : 17) and
share with Him the awe-inspiring privilege of calling
our Creator " Abba! Father!" By nature man is a
servant of God and must call Him " Lord "; and now by
grace he has become a " new creature," a heavenly
creature who is able to call Him " Father." St. Thomas

Aquinas taught that the gift of grace in a single man is a greater and more noble work of God than the excellence of the whole of natural creation.[4]

Grace is a ray of divine light, a heavenly beauty filling the soul and stamping it with Christ's image through the seal of the Holy Ghost. The man in grace shares the divine nature, receives divine privileges, eternity, happiness, perfection, and holiness. It binds a man to God in a way we could never have imagined possible but for His revelation, making us children of the heavenly Father, brothers and sisters of Christ—dying and rising with Him and sharing His inheritance. The man in grace knows that God is his Father, and heaven is his home ; he knows that Christ is his brother Who went before him to prepare him a dwelling place ; that grace is only the " first fruits " of the Holy Ghost to be followed by full redemption of body and soul, eternal happiness and a share in the glory of God. Grace is the pledge of the beatific vision and the man filled with true hope of this eternal happiness carries the seed of heaven in his heart.

Holiness is the highest attribute of God. It is an attribute which He alone possesses as a right. In his own nature man can be good, upright, moral, but never holy. The highest angel is not holy by nature. The angels who stand before God's majesty cover their faces and never cease to cry: " Holy, holy, holy is the Lord of hosts." The word ' holy ' has tended to become devalued and is used to describe virtue and piety but in reality God alone is holy—and yet we are also made holy through grace which incorporates us into Christ as the branch into the vine stem. The life of grace *is* the life of Christ. In the Mystical Body, Head and members share the same life, the same holiness.

PREPARATION FOR JUSTIFICATION

Trent teaches us that God prepares the soul of an adult for Justification by an offer of actual grace, a call to repentance. " The purpose of this call is that they

who are turned away from God by sin may, awakened
and assisted by His grace, be disposed to turn to their
own justification by freely assenting to and co-
operating with that grace.   The result is that, when
God touches the heart of man with the illumination of
the Holy Ghost, the man who accepts that inspiration
certainly does something, since he could reject it ; on
the other hand, by his own free will, without God's
grace, he could not take one step towards justice in
God's sight."[5]

The justified sinner receives the theological virtues
of Faith, Hope and Charity with the gift of sanctifying
grace.   But Faith is not only a theological virtue infused
with grace but a necessary preparation for its reception.
Faith is the first step which the sinner must take on the
road to grace.   Without it the second step is impossible.
It alone can prompt us to look for grace and find it.
Faith is the morning star that shines in the darkness of
our souls without which we cannot come to God.   " And
without faith it is impossible to please Him.   For who-
ever would draw near to God must believe that He exists
and that He rewards those who seek Him " (Heb. 11:6).
This text is cited by the Council of Trent which teaches
that adults who have freely co-operated with the grace
of God's initial call, still assisted by divine grace, " con-
ceive faith from hearing, and they are freely led to God.
They believe that the divine revelation and promises are
true, especially that the unjustified man is justified by
God's grace ' through the redemption which is in Christ
Jesus ' (Rom. 3:24)."[6]   The gift of faith can still exist
in a man who has forfeited sanctifying grace by mortal
sin for which he is unrepentant.   Such a faith, however,
is a dead faith and remains dead until the sinner repents.

The Council of Trent explains that, having acknowledged their sinful state through faith in divine revelation,
sinners: " by turning from a salutary fear of divine
justice to a consideration of God's mercy . . . are en-
couraged to hope, trusting that God will be merciful to
them for Christ's sake.   They begin to love God as the
source of all justice and are thereby moved by a sort of
hatred and detestation for sin, that is by the repentance

that must take place before baptism. Finally, they determine to receive baptism, begin a new life, and keep the divine commandments."[7]

The meaning of justification has already been explained and, as was stressed by the Council of Trent, it is not simply the remission of sins but the sanctification and renewal of the interior man. Indeed, the distinction which can be made between justification and sanctification is, to a certain extent, theoretical: the gift of sanctifying grace clearly sanctifies the sinner as its name implies. The great difference between the Catholic and Protestant theology of grace is, as will be made clear in the next chapter, that the former explains grace as sòmething positive inhering in the soul of the justified man which he did not possess in his unjustified condition. It is a *positive* quality which makes him pleasing to God *in himself* for he has " put on" Christ. The Reformers denied this.

TRANSFORMATION BY GRACE

No possible analogy can even begin to convey an adequate idea of the transformation of the soul by grace. An iron thrust in the fire remains iron yet takes on new qualities beyond its normal range—heat, light, burning power. There is a fable of the common briar into which was budded the stem of a royal rose. When June came it bore fragrant roses of great beauty and, passing by, the gardener smiled and said: " Your beauty is not due, dear briar, to that which came from you but to that which I put into you." The marvel of God's grace in His people is not due to what they were by nature, wild briars, but to what He put into them—Christ Himself, the source and cause of grace and its first and greatest gift.

Justified men, Trent teaches us, whether they have continuously kept grace, or lost it and recovered it again, " should consider these words of the Apostle: ' Abound in every good work, knowing that your labour is not vain in the Lord ' (1 Cor. 15:58) ; ' for God is not unjust that He should forget your work and the love you have shown His name ' (Heb. 10:35)."[8]   Faith without good works is dead, as St. James makes clear: " What does it profit, my brethren, if a man says he has faith but has not works?   Can his faith save him?   If a brother or sister is ill-clad and in lack of daily food, and one of you says to them, ' Go in peace, be warmed and filled,' without giving them the things needed for the body, what does it profit?   So faith by itself, if it has no works is dead " (James 2:14-17).

Although justification itself, the gift of sanctifying grace, cannot be merited, justified men can merit an increase in grace by good works.   This increase is not *produced* by their efforts alone ; God grants it freely as a reward.   The Reformers denied such a possibility as they claimed that it would make God man's debtor, clearly an impossible situation.   But there are two ways by which we can justly expect recompense of another: by having done him a service which puts him under an obligation to us or because he had previously promised us a reward if we performed certain actions.   It is in the latter respect that we can merit an increase of grace, because it is a reward freely offered by a bountiful Lord. St. Paul clearly believed that he would receive such a reward when he wrote: " I have fought the good fight, I have finished the race, I have kept the faith.   Henceforth there is laid up for me the crown of righteousness, which the Lord, the righteous judge, will award to me on that Day, and not only to me but to all who have loved His appearing " (2 Tim. 4:7, 8).   The words " crown of righteousness " and " righteous judge " express very forcibly the idea of a recompense which has been merited and is due in justice.   As the Council of Trent explains: " Christ promises even to the person who gives a drink of cold water to one of His least ones that he shall not be without his reward " (Matt. 10:42).[9] The teaching of the Church as defined by this Council is that good works done with the help of God by one who is a living member of Christ truly merit increase of grace and the life eternal.

GOOD WORKS IN CHRIST

The good works of a justified man are by no means something done in isolation from Christ for which he can claim a purely personal credit.   They are meritorious only and precisely because they are in a very real sense Christ's actions, activities of the new divine life of grace. It is not for us to boast as Christ brings forth the fruit. (Rom. 3:27).

Christ has made Himself the Head of the new humanity; He wishes to make of redeemed mankind one Body and thus make it the extension and fulfilment of Himself.   Grace is life in Christ—the good works of a member of the Mystical Body are done with Christ, for the life of grace is a life of co-operation between Christ and His members.   " As the branch cannot bear fruit by itself, unless it abides in the vine, neither can you unless you abide in Me.   I am the vine, you are the branches.   He who abides in Me, and I in him, he it is that bears much fruit, for apart from Me you can do nothing . . . By this My Father is glorified, that you bear much fruit, and so prove to be My disciples " (Jn. 15:4, 5, 8).   Nor are our good works done in isolation from the other members of the Mystical Body, incorporation into Christ incorporates us into all His members, that fellowship of grace which we call the Church.   The ultimate end of Holy Communion is not simply the union of the individual soul with Christ but the unity of the Mystical Body.

Pope St. Leo said in a Christmas sermon:

" Let us thank God the Father through His Son in the Holy Ghost, who took pity on us in the great love He bore us, and Who, when we were dead in sin, gave us life in and with Christ, that in Him we might become a new creature, newly fashioned.   Let us renounce our old selves and all that we did then, and having received a share in the Sonship of Christ let us put away the works of the flesh. *Christians, recognise your dignity,* and having received a share in the divine nature, beware of falling back into your former lowliness.   Consider

Whose Body it is of which you are a member, and Who its Head. Remember how you were snatched from darkness and set in God's kingdom of light. Through the sacrament of Baptism you have become a temple of the Holy Ghost. Beware of driving out so great a Guest by your sinful deeds and subjecting yourselves once more to the slavery of the devil. For your ransom was the Blood of Christ. He will judge you in justice, Who redeemed you in mercy."[10]

Chapter III

SOLA FIDES JUSTIFICAT
(The Protestant Doctrine of Justification by Faith Alone)

" If this doctrine falls it is all over with us "
—Martin Luther, *Table Talk*

ALL THAT is intended here is to outline the broad
principles of the Protestant doctrine as taught by the
leading Reformers. There were, of course, differences
of opinion among them and, especially in the case of
Luther, it is not always clear what was being taught.
As is normally the case with sects when they begin to
sub-divide, their internal disputes eventually become
more fierce than their opposition to the body from which
they have broken away. Calvinism expanded not
simply at the expense of Catholics but of Lutherans in
North Germany and the name *Reformed* first came into
common use when opposed not to Catholics but to
Lutherans.[1] Before 1570, some stricter Lutherans had
even begun to profess that Catholicism was nearer to
orthodoxy than Calvinism.[2]

While Luther himself did not actually go to the extent
of totally rejecting the Catholic system, such a rejection
was inevitable if his principles were pursued to their
logical conclusion. It is also taken for granted that the
basic thesis of the Continental Reformers concerning
Justification was adopted by Cranmer and his associates.
This is proved beyond doubt both from his own works
and the authoritative studies of the period.[3]

The Catholic Church teaches that original sin has
resulted in a wounding of our nature which sets up in
the soul a resistance to good. " For the good which I
will I do not ; but the evil which I will not, that I do "

(Rom. 7:19). But a soul which is willing to accept the assistance of God's grace can still refrain from sin.

Luther taught that through the Fall of Adam man's nature had become essentially evil, and must ever remain evil ; that human nature was a mass of corruption and even the Redeeming Blood of Christ does not cleanse or heal it: man can contribute absolutely nothing to his own salvation. God justifies us by transferring the guilt which made us liable to punishment to the head of His own Son. Calvin was explicit on this point: " Our acquittal is this—that the guilt which made us liable to punishment was transferred to the head of the Son of God (Isaias 52:12). We must especially remember this substitution in order that we may not be all our lives in trepidation and anxiety, as if the vengeance which the Son of God transferred to Himself, were still impending over us."[4] Christ has taken the punishment of sinners upon Himself, expiating their sins with His Blood and appeasing the Father. Although the soul of the sinner is *not* cleansed, the merits won by Christ are applied to him and his sins are ignored or overlooked by God. The souls of sinners *remain hideous in themselves* but are covered with the cloak of Christ's righteousness. As was explained in Chapter 1, for the Reformers, the substitutionary punishment of Christ on the gibbet in place of guilty mankind paid the penalty demanded by divine vindicatory justice. Christ was " put to the torture by God and so took upon Himself God's anger." As a result of this *penal substitution* of Christ for sinners, the elect, that is those whom God has predestined for salvation, no longer have their sins imputed to them. The merits of Christ are imputed to them in place of their sins. Man becomes just in the sight of God *simply by non-imputation of sin.* There was no question of an inner sanctification which blots out sin and justifies the sinner before God, effected by the co-operation of the sinner with grace *mediated* through a sacramental system by means of which the merits won for us upon Calvary were mediated to men through a Church which is the prolongation of the Incarnation in time. To quote Cranmer: " Christ him-

self in his own person made a sacrifice for our sins upon
the cross . . . And the benefit hereof is in no man's
power to give unto any other, but every man must
receive it at Christ's hands himself, by his own faith
and belief . . ."⁵   For a Protestant, Justification means
declaring a man to be just: for a Catholic, it means
making him so.⁶   For a Protestant the souls of St.
Francis of Assissi or St. Thérèse of Lisieux are masses
of corruption hidden beneath the cloak of Christ's
righteousness: for a Catholic their souls are pleasing to
God in themselves, having become so through the indwelling of sanctifying grace—made possible and
intensified by their own free co-operation.

Grace for the Reformers was not something *in* man
but was external to the soul altogether. It existed only
in God's divine will ; it was a sentence passed by the
Divine Judge imputing Christ's righteousness to the
elect. Justification was not an inner change by which
a soul became a sacred thing but a mere non-imputation
of sins. Faith meant not a firm acceptance of divine
revelation (see Chapter II) but the individual's personal
conviction that the merits of Christ had been applied
to him. The sinner " is delivered from the punishment
due to sin, but not from sin itself."⁷

Luther overthrew a system of belief developed over
fifteen centuries on the basis of his personal interpretation of Romans 1:17 which states, in a literal translation, that " the just man will live by faith."   His
interpretation could not possibly be reconciled with the
Second Epistle of James, cited in the previous chapter—
then this epistle must be rejected as an " epistle of
straw," once again on the personal authority of Luther.⁸
Faith was all that counted ; good works were of no avail
—indeed, they were impossible since all man's actions
were made evil by the source from which they sprang—
human nature, which was *essentially corrupt* as a result
of Original Sin.

" Luther tells us we must give up trying to escape
sin," writes Henri Rondet. " We have to abandon ourselves to God, worry no longer about ourselves, consider ourselves incapable of cure, and throw ourselves

on the divine mercy. God cannot change the heart of
men. But he can close his eyes and act as though man's
heart were changed. He can consider the sinner as
just and cover him with Christ's merits as with a cloak.
Sin will remain and will not be destroyed, but it will no
longer be imputed. Hence, it is pointless to worry any
longer about works. External practices and concern
over perfection are nothing but Pharisaism. We act
like mercenaries in wanting to conquer heaven with our
feeble blows. Man simply cannot merit before God.
Grace then, is the certainty we have concerning a God
who looks upon a sinful man as though he were just.
God favours man and considers him as holy because of
the merits of the Redeemer."[9]

In fairness to the Reformers, it should be emphasised
that at no time have the mainstream of Protestants
interpreted the doctrine of Justification as a licence to
sin. They have taken a godly life to be a mark of the
elect. There have, of course, been some extreme sects
which have taken the doctrine to what they felt was
its logical conclusion, in other words, that anything is
permitted.

The concept of the Church mediating grace through
the Sacraments was anathema to the Reformers. It was
axiomatic to their theology that nothing man could do,
no priestly power, nor anything in the created universe
could work any good in the order of salvation or
produce any intrinsic effects in man's soul. The
" grace " of Justification was held to be essentially the
favour of the divine will and no Church, no priest, could
play any efficacious part in mediating that grace to
others. " The doctrine of a sacrificing priesthood whose
ministry was an objective means of helping Christian
souls to reach a right relationship with God was resented
by the Reformers as an intolerable intrusion into the
inviolable sanctuary of saving faith where each man
experienced his personal assurance of grace."[10] The
divine decree of acquittal, once made, was absolute.
Once a man had been justified through the saving merits
of Christ his salvation was assured. The sacrifice which
made it possible for Christ's merits to be imputed to

the elect was past. It could be commemorated in a thankful memorial which could stir up the faith of the elect but, and this is axiomatic to the Protestant doctrine, the elect received their justification *directly from God.*

The inevitable result of the acceptance of Justification by Faith was perfectly summarised by the German scholar F. Arnold when he says that it: " struck at the heart of the Catholic sacramental system in general and of the Mass in particular."[11] The Reformers could not eliminate all the sacraments " but they got rid of five out of the seven and then stripped the two that remained of any intrinsic value or force. The whole ' work ' was done by the recipient. He arrived with the trust in God to which the word ' faith ' was attached, and on the grounds of that faith good was accomplished within him."[12] The most evident and most spectacular changes, wrote Mgr. Hughes, " were, of course, the alterations in the public services of religion. These were the changes which made the immediate—and generally hostile—impression on contemporaries ; and it is these which have chiefly occupied the controversialists of our own time. But even more important was the new basic theory of religion which these changes presupposed, and from which they sprang."[13] The Reformers rightly sensed that the Mass lay at the heart of the Catholic faith and that the destruction of the Mass was of greater priority than that of the papacy, for in destroying the Mass they would " tear out the heart from the body of the Church."[14] The hatred which the Reformers felt for the Mass will be illustrated in detail in Chapter V. Francis Clark expresses the opinion that, after a reading of Luther's *Babylonian Captivity* of 1520, ". . . it is clear that Luther's rejection of the sacrifice of the altar stemmed naturally from his first and central intuition: that is, from his gospel of Justification by Faith alone, from the opposition he proclaimed between the word of God which heralds from on high the divine decree of pardon to men, who can do nothing but receive it, and on the other hand the objective efficacy of the Catholic sacramental system, by

which grace is mediated to men so that they participate
in divine life, and by which the Church, her priests and
members are privileged to have an active share in
Christ's power of conveying that life to others."[15]

The Mass, claimed the Reformers, was no sacrifice,
" nor yet good work ; but a blasphemous profanation of
the Lord's Holy Supper, a manifest wickedness, an
horrible idolatry, and a foul abomination."[16]   " Away
therefore with their abominable doctrine that the sacrifice of the Mass is the principal means to apply Christ's
death to the quick and the dead: wherein all men may
see that they lie boldly."[17]

Chapter IV

CATHOLIC TEACHING ON THE EUCHARIST

" Christ is offered today and He Himself as priest, offers Himself in order that He may remit our sins."
—St. Ambrose.[1]

THE EUCHARIST is the centre of Christian life just as Christ is the central figure in the Christian religion. As well as being a sacrifice, It is the greatest of all the sacraments as It contains Christ Himself while in the other Sacraments Christ acts and applies the merits of His Passion for a particular purpose. St. Thomas Aquinas points out that all the other Sacraments are ordained to this Sacrament as to their end.[2] It not only represents the Passion and death of Christ but contains it—the Mass *is* the sacrifice of the Cross.[3] " The Passion of the Lord is the sacrifice we offer," wrote St. Cyprian.[4] " The priests of the Church are ordained not primarily to preach the gospel, not merely to comfort the sick with the consoling truths of religion, not merely to take the lead in works of social improvement, but to offer the Sacrifice of the Mass, to consecrate the Eucharist."[5] It would be impossible to write anything which could exaggerate the importance of the Eucharist. Catholics in the past have thought nothing in art, riches and architecture too beautiful to lavish upon their churches because they contain the King of kings Himself ; and even the poorest have been ready to deprive themselves of the necessities of life to support their clergy so that at whatever cost the Sacrifice of the Mass should continue to be offered. Devotion to the Eucharist is not an incidental pious practice—it is the very essence of Catholic life.[6]

" By sacrifice man offers himself and his life to God, his sovereign Lord and Creator ; by the Sacraments God gives Himself, He gives us a participation of His own divine life, to man. In sacrifice a stream of homage flows from man to the eternal Source of all being ; by the sacraments grace, santification, descends in copious flood upon the souls of men. This two-fold stream from God to man and from man to God, flows swift and strong in the Eucharist, Sacrament and Sacrifice. As the culminating act in the life of Jesus Christ on earth was the sacrifice He offered on Calvary to His eternal Father, so the central act of Catholic worship in the Church, the Mystical Body of Christ, is the Eucharistic Sacrifice, the Mass which He instituted to be a perpetual com-memoration and renewal of it. Likewise, just as it was through the sacred humanity of Christ that God merci-fully deigned to transmit to us the divine life of grace, so the Sacrament of the Eucharist, which truly contains that living and life-giving humanity, holds the principal place among the Sacraments instituted by Christ for our sanctification.

" Truly, really and substantially present upon the altar under the appearance of bread and wine, Christ our High Priest offers Himself, the infinite Victim, to His Father through the ministry of His priests. This is indeed a sacrifice unto the odour of sweetness, in which Christ, God and man, offers to His Father an infinite adoration, a prayer of unbounded efficacy, propitiation and satisfaction superabundantly sufficient for the sins of all mankind, thanksgiving in a unique manner pro-portionate to God's unstinted generosity to men. And then, as if it were in munificent answer to this infinitely pleasing gift which through Christ man has made to God, there comes God's best gift to man: the all holy Victim, divinely accepted and ratified, is set before men to be their heavenly food. Through Christ we have given ourselves to God. Through Christ God gives His own life to us, that we may be made partakers of His divinity. The Victim of the Eucharistic Sacrifice, offered to man under the form of food, is the august Sacrament of the Eucharist."[7]

Pope Leo XIII condemned as being in serious error those who rejected the sacrifice of the Mass on the grounds that " it derogated from the reality and efficacy of the sacrifice wrought by Christ when He was nailed to the Cross ' offered once for all to drain the cup of the world's sins ' (Heb. 9:28). That expiation for sin was wholly perfect and complete ; *nor is it in any way another expiation but the very same, that is present in the Eucharistic Sacrifice* . . . It was the divine plan of the Redeemer that the sacrifice consummated once upon the Cross should be perpetual and perennial. It is made perpetual in the most Holy Eucharist, which brings not merely a figure or an empty commemoration of the reality *but the reality itself* although under a different appearance."[8]

Fr. Joseph Jungmann writes: " When Christ on the Cross cried out His *Consummatum est,* few were the men who noticed it, fewer still the men who perceived that this phrase announced a turning point for mankind, that this death opened into everlasting life gates through which, from that moment on, all the peoples of the earth would pass. Now, to meet the expectant longing of mankind, this great event is arrested and, through Christ's institution held fast for these coming generations so that they might be conscious witnesses of that event even in the latest centuries and amongst the remotest nations, and might look up to it in holy rapture."[9]

Despite the fact that at every Mass Jesus Christ is the High Priest Who offers the Sacrifice it is most certainly a work, something in which men play a part and which contributes to their salvation. The Mass is not only the Sacrifice of Christ but the Sacrifice of the Church. The Sacrifice can *only* be offered through the ministry of His priests. It is an aspect of the mystery referred to in Chapter I, of the fact that Christ requires the members of His Mystical Body ; that He has willed to save mankind with their help. Not only are the graces won by Christ applied through the efforts of men but it is not Christ alone Who is offered in the Mass—we are required to offer ourselves as victims

with Him.[10] " As the Church is the body of this head,"
wrote St. Augustine, " through Him She learns to offer
Herself."[11] Furthermore, although the intrinsic value
of the Sacrifice of the Mass, like that of the Cross, is
infinite, Christ being both High Priest and Sacrificial
Victim, its extrinsic value is limited as regards the
fruits of any particular Mass. The value of a particular
Mass " is dependent on the greater or lesser holiness of
the reigning Pope, the bishops and the clergy throughout the world. The holier the Church in Her members
(especially the Pope and the Episcopate), the more agree-
able must be Her sacrifice in the eyes of God . . . With
Christ and the Church is associated in the third place
the celebrating priest, the representative through whom
Christ offers up the Sacrifice. If he be a man of great
personal devotion, and purity, there will accrue an
additional fruit, which will benefit himself and those in
whose favour he applies the Mass. Hence the faithful
are guided by a sound instinct when they prefer to have
the Mass celebrated by an upright and holy priest rather
than by an unworthy one . . . In the fourth place must
be mentioned those who take an active part in the Mass,
e.g., the servers, sacristan, organist, singers and, finally
the whole congregation."[12] Needless to say, the application of the fruits of the Mass to the living for whom
it is offered or who participate in it will be governed by
their own dispositions (see Appendix I). " This lack of
dispositions cannot exist in the case of the suffering
souls in Purgatory, and with them, therefore, the desired
effect, whether it be the alleviation of their sufferings,
or the shortening of their time of purgation, must in-
fallibly be produced."[13] The effectiveness of the fruits
in their case will be governed only by the holiness and
fervour of the Church as a whole and Her particular
members involved in offering this particular Mass.

Once the Protestant leaders " had adopted the doctrine
of justification by faith only, and had thrown over the
reality of sanctifying grace as the supernatural life of the
soul, there was nothing for it but to give up belief in
operative and grace-producing sacraments. So the Real
Presence and Transubstantiation had to go, and the

Eucharist had to lose altogether its sacrificial character and to be retained simply as a memorial of the Last Supper whereby the soul is moved to prayer and enabled in some way to enter into communion with and to receive Jesus Christ . . . Hence it is not surprising that, to a great extent, *belief in the Mass became the touchstone of Catholic orthodoxy* and that all through the centuries of controversy with Protestantism, Catholic theologians should have used all their powers of argument and all their resources of learning in its defence."[14]

The teaching that every Mass produced fruits which the celebrant could apply to both the living and the dead was above all else what evoked the fury of the Reformers. This was the " good work " par excellence. It was quite incompatible with their doctrine of Justification and must therefore be rejected, as will be made clear in Chapter VII.

There can be no doubt that the Protestant heresiarchs fully realised that it was the Mass that mattered. It was upon the Mass that they directed the full force of their attack.

Mysterium Fidei by *Bernadette Keenan*

Chapter V

THE MOST HORRIBLE BLASPHEMY

THE USE of the word "Reformers" is something of a misnomer for the Protestant heresiarchs. It has become the standard usage in histories of the Reformation, another misnomer, but it does not require a very deep study to realise that they were not reformers but revolutionaries—men out to overthrow the existing religion and replace it with one which they had fabricated themselves on the grounds that it conformed with the teaching and practice of primitive Christianity.[1] Once they had gained power they tried to inspire in the simple Faithful the same hatred of the Church of Christ which inspired their own fanatical zeal. They were religious revolutionaries, and with perfect revolutionary insight they sensed that the first step in consolidating their power was to inspire hatred of the old order. The old religion, the people were told, is "the idolatrous church . . . being indeed not only a harlot (as the Scripture calleth her) but also a foul, filthy, old withered harlot (for she is indeed of ancient years) . . . the foulest and filthiest harlot that ever was seen . . . the great strumpet of all strumpets, the mother of all strumpets, the mother of whoredom set forth by St. John in his Revelation . . ."[2]

They correctly sensed, not surprisingly as they had almost invariably been priests, that it was the Mass that mattered: that it was against the Mass rather than the Papacy that the brunt of their attack must be launched.[3] This point is stressed by Dr. J. Lortz in his book *Die Reformation in Deutschland*.[4] One of the most outstanding and perceptive contemporary champions of the Mass was the German theologian John

Cochlaeus (1479-1552).   He rightly pointed out that in
attacking the Mass Luther was attacking Christ Himself " since He is the true founder and perfector of the
Mass, the true High Priest of the Mass and also the
One Who is sacrificed as all Christian teachers acknowledge."5   With equal accuracy he diagnosed the contradiction which lay at the heart of the heresiarchs'
claim to be " reformers."   " They are justly deemed
guilty of heresy who instead of seeking remedies for
what is amiss, set themselves to abolish the very substance on account of the abuse."6   He warned his fellow
Catholic apologists not to concentrate their main efforts
on defending the primacy of the Pope but on defending
the Mass, a task which was far more vital, for " thereby
Luther threatens to tear out the heart from the body of
the Church."7

The Reformers themselves were bitterly divided concerning the doctrine of the Lord's Supper, but they were
united in a common detestation of the sacrificial interpretation which had always been taught in the Catholic
Church.8   Luther was honest enough to admit the traditional nature of the teaching and the support of " the
holy Fathers, so many authorities and so widespread a
custom constantly observed throughout the world."
His answer was ". . . reject them all rather than admit
that the Mass is a work and a sacrifice . . ."9

Luther himself assessed the situation with perfect
accuracy when he stated: " once the Mass has been
overthrown, I say we'll have overthrown the whole of
Popedom."10

The hatred of the Reformers for the Mass is best
illustrated by quoting a few examples from the wealth
of material available:

LUTHER*: " I declare that all the brothels (though

---

* It is worth mentioning that on 19th July, 1970, at the
  Assembly of the World Lutheran Federation at Evian,
  Mgr. Willebrands, the Pope's envoy, proposed a toast
  to " the profoundly religious personality of Martin
  Luther and the honest self-sacrifice with which he
  sought the message of the Gospel."13

God has reproved them severely), all the manslaughters, murders, thefts and adulteries have wrought less abomination than the Popish Mass."[11]

Masses are "the height of idolatory and impiety," an evil introduced by Satan himself.

"It is indeed upon the Mass as on a rock that the whole Papal system is built, with its monasteries, its bishoprics, its collegiate churches, its altars, its ministries, its doctrine, i.e., with all its guts. All these cannot fail to crumble once their sacrilegious and abominable Mass falls."[12]

CALVIN: ". . . Satan blinded almost the whole world with the pestilential error of believing that the Mass is a sacrifice and an oblation for obtaining the remission of sins . . . This abomination of the Mass being presented in a golden vessel, that is under the name of God's word, has made all the kingdoms of the earth so drunk, so besotted and dazed from the greatest to the least, that, some more stupid than brute beasts, they have set the beginning and the end of their salvation wholly in this deadly abyss. Sure it is that Satan never devised a more effective engine for attacking and vanquishing Christ's realm."[14]

LATIMER: "We were wont to have *sacrificium missae* 'the sacrifice of the Mass'; which was the most horrible blasphemy which could be devised, for it was against the dignity of Christ and his passion; but this sacrifice of thanksgiving everyone may make."[15]

CRANMER: "But what availeth it to take away beads, pardons, pilgrimages, and such other like popery, so long as the two chief roots remain unpulled up? Whereof, so long as they remain, will spring again all former impediments of the Lord's harvest, and corruption of his flock. The rest is but branches and leaves, the cutting away whereof is but like topping and lopping of a tree, or cutting down of weeds, leaving the body standing and the roots in the ground; but the very body of the tree, or rather the roots of the weeds, is the popish doctrine of transubstantiation, of the real presence of Christ's flesh and blood in the sacrament of the altar (as they call it) and the sacrifice and oblation of Christ made by the priest, for the salvation of the quick and the dead."[16]

Pope Honorius III commanded ". . . that the 'priests would diligently teach the people from time to time, that when they lifted up the bread, called the host, the people should then bow down ; and that likewise they should do so when the priest carrieth the host unto sick folks.' These be the statutes and ordinances of Rome, under pretence of holiness, to lead the people unto all error and idolatry: not bringing them by bread unto Christ, but from Christ unto bread.

" But all that love and believe Christ himself, let them not think that Christ is corporally in the bread ; but let them lift up their hearts unto heaven, and worship him, sitting there at the right hand of his Father. Let them worship him in themselves, whose temples they be, in whom he dwelleth and liveth spiritually: but in no wise let them worship him as being corporally in the bread. For he is not in it, neither spiritually as he is in man, nor corporally, as he is in heaven, but only sacramentally, as a thing may be said to be in the figure, whereby it is signified."[17]

BULLINGER: " Moreover man needs to blind himself with these words, high mass, low mass. In the high mass are the selfsame abominations which are in the lowest. In both of them is the institution and ordinance of Christ perverted ; in both of them is he worshipped in the bread ; in both are idols served ; in both, specially in the service of the saints, is help asked of creatures ; in both of them is the wicked Canon, the greatest portion of the Mass. There is nothing in it of old antiquity, nothing of the apostolic simplicity."[18]

Chapter VI

PROTESTANT TEACHING ON THE EUCHARIST
Part 1—*The Rejection of Sacrifice*

". . . the foulest and most heinous error that was
ever imagined "—Cranmer[1]

ACCEPTANCE OF the doctrine of Justification by
Faith alone necessarily involved the rejection of the
sacrificial nature of the Mass. The Reformers taught
that the one oblation upon Calvary had appeased the
Father's anger for ever. God had granted an irrevocable decree of pardon to His predestined elect. Religion
was essentially the encounter of the individual with
God's free choice to disregard his sins and impute
Christ's righteousness to him instead.[2] "Faith in God's
promise is a matter for each one separately," wrote
Luther, "and cannot be applied or communicated to
any other."[3] This doctrine was accepted by the
English Reformers who totally rejected the Catholic
concept of the Church as an extension of the Incarnation, mediating the grace of Christ to man in every age,
above all through the Sacrifice of the Mass. "It can
hardly be pretended that in this matter of Justification
Cranmer has anything new to say. All his main points
can be paralleled in Luther and Zwingli before him as
well as Calvin and other contemporary writers," explains
Dr. G. W. Bromiley in *Thomas Cranmer Theologian*.[4]
The celebration of the Eucharist could be no more than
a *memorial* or *commemoration* of the penal sacrifice, in
the commonly accepted meaning of these words, in that
it brought the event commemorated to mind for those
present. It could have no present sacrificial efficacy.[5]

The terms *memorial* and *commemoration* are used in a perfectly orthodox sense within Catholic theology. The Mass most certainly *is* the memorial of the Lord, but it is a memorial bequeathed to us by Christ Himself when he said " Haec quotiescumque feceritis, in mei memoriam facietis." Protestants frequently hold memorial services in which the memory of some dead person is commemorated—but in traditional Catholic theology Christ's Passion is commemorated by making the Passion present, the Memorial contains the Passion, it *is* the Passion. Not so with the Protestants. " All the Reformers agree in repudiating the hitherto accepted Catholic doctrine that there is an offering of the Body and Blood of Christ by the priest in the Mass, in memory of the Passion, and that the Mass is in this sense a sacrifice."[6]

There can be no doubt whatsoever that the Reformers fully understood the doctrine they were rejecting. Cranmer was a trained theologian who knew perfectly well the value of the changes he had introduced.[7] When he died at the stake he not only repudiated all his recantations and denounced the Pope as Antichrist but repeated his Protestant doctrine of the Eucharist.[8] The clarity with which he grasped the Catholic doctrine which he rejected is made clear when he states: " But it is a wondrous thing to see what shifts and cautels the popish antichrists devise to colour and cloke their wicked errors . . . For the Papists, to excuse themselves, do say that they make no new sacrifice, nor none other sacrifice than Christ made (for they be not so blind but that they see, that then they should add another sacrifice to Christ's sacrifice, and so make his sacrifice unperfect:) but they say that they make the self-same sacrifice for sin that Christ himself made. And here they run headlong into the foulest and most heinous error that ever was imagined."[9]

John Bradford, Chaplain to Bishop Ridley, denounced the Catholic Church for lying boldly in its " abominable doctrine that the Mass is the principal means to apply Christ's death to the quick and the dead," but explained the doctrine in terms taken from contemporary Catholic theology so accurately that it would have been hard for a Catholic apologist to improve upon his summary.

" Now concerning the sacrifice, they teach that though our Saviour himself did indeed make a full and perfect sacrifice, propitiatory and satisfactory for the sins of all the whole world, never more so (that is to say bloodily) to be offered again, yet in his supper he offered the same sacrifice unto his Father but unbloodily, that is to say, in will and desire . . . which unbloody sacrifice he commanded his church to offer in remembrance of his bloody sacrifice, as the principal mean whereby his bloody sacrifice is applied both to the quick and the dead: as baptism is the mean by which regeneration is applied by the priest to the infant or child that is baptised."[10]

As well as stressing that their Lord's Supper was merely a memorial service in which Christ was remembered, the Reformers took great pains to attack the principle that it was possible for a priest to offer a Mass and obtain benefits for *other* persons either living or dead.   The belief that a Mass could benefit *other* persons, particularly the souls in Purgatory, was the epitomization of the concept of the " good work " which, if accepted, ruled out their doctrine of Justification, and if that fell everything fell.

Thus Luther: " In the institution of the Lord's Supper, Christ does not command priests to offer for other living and dead persons . . . It is much more absurd that the Mass is applied to freeing the souls of the dead, for the Mass was instituted to be a recollection, that is, that those who use the Lord's Supper may by the remembrance of the benefit of Christ, establish and strengthen their faith, and comfort their terrified consciences. . . ."[11]

These principles can clearly be discerned in the writing of Cranmer. " Christ himself in his own person made a sacrifice for our sins upon the cross . . . and so did never no priest, man, nor creature but he, nor he did the same never more than once. And the benefit hereof is in no man's power to give unto any other, but every man must receive it at Christ's hands himself, by his own faith and belief . . ."[12]

And again: ". . . the offering of the priest in the mass, or the appointing of his ministration at his pleasure, to them that be quick or dead, cannot merit and deserve, neither to himself, nor to them to whom he singeth or saith, the remission of their sins ; but such popish doctrine is contrary to the doctrine of the gospel and injurious to the sacrifice of Christ. For if only the death of Christ be the oblation, sacrifice, and price wherefore our sins be pardoned, then the act or ministration of the priest cannot have the same office. Wherefore it is an *abominable blasphemy* to give that office or dignity to a priest, which pertaineth only to Christ ; or to affirm that the church hath need of any such sacrifice: as who should say, that Christ's sacrifice were not sufficient for the remission of our sins, or else that his sacrifice should hang upon the sacrifice of a priest.

"But all such priests as pretend to be Christ's successors in making a sacrifice of him, they be his most *heinous and horrible adversaries.* For never no person made a sacrifice of Christ, but he himself only . . . all popish priests that presume to make every day a sacrifice of Christ, either must they needs make Christ's sacrifice vain, unperfect, and unsufficient, or else is their sacrifice in vain which is added to the sacrifice which is already of itself sufficient and perfect."[13]

This viewpoint is put even more forcefully by John Hooper, Bishop of Gloucester, in *A Brief and Clear Confession of the Christian Faith.* "I believe that the holy Supper of the Lord is not a sacrifice, but only a remembrance and commemoration of this holy sacrifice of Jesus Christ. Therefore it ought not to be worshipped as God, neither is Christ therein contained ; who must be worshipped in faith only, without all corruptible elements. Likewise I believe and confess that the popish Mass is an invention and ordinance of man, a *sacrifice of Antichrist,* and a forsaking of the sacrifice of Jesus Christ, that is to say, of his death and passion ; and that it is *a stinking and infected sepulchre,* which hideth and covereth the merit of the blood of Christ ; and therefore ought the Mass to be abolished, and the holy Supper of the Lord to be restored and set in his perfection again."[14]

This belief that "the holy Supper of the Lord" is only a memorial in the commonly accepted sense of the word was insisted upon by the Reformers time and again. ". . . his holy Supper was ordained for this purpose, that every man, eating and drinking thereof, should remember that Christ died for him, and so should exercise his faith, and comfort himself by the remembrance of Christ's benefits, and so give unto Christ most hearty thanks, and give himself also clearly unto him."[15]

The Reformers do, on occasions, use such words as offering, sacrifice, and even oblation—but always in a sense which is diametrically opposed to the use of these words in Catholic theology, just as is the case with such expressions as "sacramental presence," the bread being Christ's "Body" and the wine His "Blood," or a "consecration" of the bread and wine. These terms will be examined more closely in Chapter VII.

Cranmer explains that there is "Another kind of sacrifice . . . which doth not reconcile us to God, but is made of them that be reconciled by Christ, to testify our duties unto God, and to shew ourselves thankful unto him. And therefore they be called sacrifices of laud, praise, and thanksgiving."[16] This "sacrifice of laud and praise" consists of "the humble confession of all penitent hearts, their acknowledging of Christ's benefits, their thanksgiving for the same, their faith and consolation in Christ, their humble submission and obedience to God's will and commandments . . ."[17]

In contrast with this the Mass "is neither a sacrifice propitiatory, nor yet a sacrifice of laud and praise, nor in any wise allowed before God, but abominable and detestable . . ."[18]

The leading Anglican liturgist of recent times, Professor Ratcliff, writes that in the *First Prayer Book* Cranmer "had abandoned belief in the traditional doctrine of the sacrifice of the Mass and held that Christian sacrifice as taught in Scripture consisted in the oblation of praise and thanksgiving and the offering of ourselves."[19]   As Mgr. Hughes explains, Cranmer hated the theology of the Mass as passionately as if it were a living enemy.[20]   His doctrine, which was the doctrine of the generality of the Reformers, is summed up by Fr. Messenger in terms which correspond exactly with Professor Ratcliff's description: ". . . in the Holy Communion there is a ' sacrifice ' of praise and thanksgiving, and an ' offering ' of ourselves.   There is also a ' commemoration and remembrance ' i.e. recalling to mind, of the Sacrifice of the Cross.   *But there is no offering of Christ either by priest or people.*"[21]   This is also the precise judgement of our bishops in their vindication of *Apostolicae Curae* in 1898.   They insist that the only " sacrifice " in which Cranmer believed was " a sacrifice in which the person offering is not an earthly representative of Christ, or the thing offered the Body and Blood of Christ, but the offerers are the Christian people acting in their own name, and the thing offered is themselves, through their praise and thanksgiving for the benefit of redemption, their obedience to God's Law, and their subjugation of all evil passions."[22]

The Protestant conception of the " Supper of the Lord " necessitated immediate and drastic action wherever they could gain the support of those exercising political control of a country.   " And forasmuch as in such masses is manifest wickedness and idolatry, wherein the priest alone maketh oblation satisfactory, and applieth the same for the quick and the dead at his will and pleasure, all such popish masses are to be clearly taken away out of christian churches, and the true use of the Lord's Supper is to be restored again ; wherein godly people assembled together may receive the sacrament every man for himself, to declare that he remembereth what benefit he hath received by the death of Christ, and to testify that he is a member of Christ's body, fed with his flesh, and drinking his blood spiritually."[23]

This restoration of " the true use of the Lord's Supper " was to be achieved both by using those parts of the Catholic Mass which could be interpreted in a Protestant sense and by the addition of completely new formulas added under the guise of a "restoration of primitive Christianity," a return to what the Reformers regarded as "primitive purity and simplicity, in contrast to the corruption and error of later Catholic times."[24]

The Protestant rejection of the sacrificial nature of the Mass clearly necessitated a rejection of the Catholic concept of the priesthood. Where there was no victim and no sacrifice there was no necessity for a priest. "Just as Cranmer has devised a communion rite which was free of all idea of sacrifice in the true sense of that word, so he removed from the ordination rite for priests all mention of the power of consecration."[25]

In their vindication of *Apostolicae Curae*, the Catholic bishops explain that "there was no place in Cranmer's system for any doctrine which could recognise in the Christian ministry a power of consecrating and offering the Body of Christ, and could require an ordinal suited to convey it. He would have been flagrantly inconsistent with himself had he conceived otherwise of the Christian minister than as one *possessing only the same powers as the layman,* but placed over the people in the interests of public order, to rule them, to instruct them, and to lead their devotions."[26]

Cranmer teaches that the difference between priest and layman is not that the priest alone has the power to offer sacrifice "and distribute and apply it as him liketh. Christ made no such difference, but the difference that is between the priest and the layman in this matter *is only in the ministration;* that the priest as a common minister of the church, doth minister and distribute the Lord's supper unto other, and other receive it at his hands. But the very supper itself was by Christ instituted and given to the whole church, not to be offered and eaten of the priest for other men, but by him to be delivered to all that would duly ask it.

" As in a prince's house the officers and ministers prepare the table, and yet other, as well as they, eat the meat and drink the drink ; so do the priests and ministers prepare the Lord's supper, read the gospel, and rehearse Christ's words, but all the people say thereto, Amen. All remember Christ's death, all give thanks to God, all repent and offer themselves an oblation to Christ, all take him for their Lord and Saviour, and spiritually feed upon him, and in token thereof they eat the bread and drink the wine in his mystical supper."[27]

In other words, the Minister was not a priest but a president, a man who possessed no powers denied to the remainder of the congregation, but simply acted as their representative by presiding over their communion service and distributing the bread and wine.

Edmund Plowden was said to be the greatest and most honest lawyer practising during the reign of Elizabeth I. The Queen admired him so much that she even offered him the Lord Chancellorship if he would renounce his Catholic faith. Plowden declined the bribe. On one occasion when he was defending a client accused of hearing Mass he elicited the fact that the rite had been performed by an *agent provocateur* masquerading as a priest. "The case is altered!" he snapped. "No priest, no Mass!"[28].

The attitude of the English Reformers towards the sacrificial nature of the Mass is perfectly expressed in Article Thirty-Two of the Forty-Two Articles of 1553 which were basically the work of Cranmer.[29] "The offring of Christe made ones for euer, is the perfecte redemption, the pacifiying of goddes displeasure, and satisfaction for al the sinnes of the whole worlde, bothe original and actuall: and there is none other satisfaction for sinne, but that alone. Wherefore the sacrifices of masses, in whiche, it was commonlie saied, that the Prieste did offre Christe for the quicke and the dead, to haue remission of peine or sinne, were forged fables, and dangerouse deceiptes."[30]

Incredible as it may seem, some Anglicans who wished to restore Catholic belief to the Church of England, have argued that this article (now Article Thirty-One) was not aimed against the sacrifice of the Mass itself, a point of view which has been endorsed by some irenical Catholics.   While there is no possible room for ambiguity in the wording of the article itself, even had there been, the only honest course would have been to interpret it in the light of the beliefs of those who had framed it, and these have been made amply clear in this chapter.   A more detailed examination of Article XXXI will be found in Appendix II.

Fol. cxxj.

✤ THE SVPPER ✤

of the Lorde, and the holy Communion, commonly called the Masse.

As many as intende to bee partakers of the holy Communion, shall sygnifie their names to the Curate, ouer night: or els in the mornyng, afore the beginning of Matins, or immediatly after.

And if any of those be an open and notorious euill liuer, so that the congregacion by hym is offended, or haue doen any wrong to his neighbours, by worde, or dede: The Curate shall call hym, and aduertise hym, in any wise not to presume to the lordes table, vntill he haue openly declared hymselfe, to haue truly repented, and amended his former naughtie life: that the congregacion maie thereby be satisfied, whiche afore were offended: and that he haue recompensed the parties, whom he hath dooen wrong vnto, or at the least bee in full purpose so to doo, as sone as he conueniently maie.

The Supper of the Lorde, and the Holy Communion, commonly called the Masse: *the opening paragraph of the Communion Service in the 1549 Book of Common Prayer*

The Bull Against Luther

Chapter VII

PROTESTANT TEACHING ON THE EUCHARIST
Part 2—*The Rejection of Transubstantiation*

" For they teach, that Christ is in the bread and
wine: but we say (according to the truth), that he
is in them that worthily eat and drink the bread
and wine . . ."—Cranmer[1]

MOST OF the Reformers accompanied their rejection of
the sacrificial nature of the Mass by the rejection of
any real, objective presence of Christ in the consecrated
elements. As is so often the case with revolutionaries
in any sphere, it is easier to discover what they reject
than what they propose to put in its place. Professor
Owen Chadwick, while explaining how Zwingli considered the sacraments to be simply signs of a covenant
between God and man, and not a means of grace,
remarks that: " In his early years as a reformer he
and his friend Oecolampadius of Basle were so engaged
on saying what the Lord's Supper was not, that they
rarely and reluctantly attempted to describe what it
was."[2]

The belief that Christ was in any way contained *in*
the consecrated elements was rejected by all the Continental and British Reformers but for Luther. Their
standpoint was clearly expressed by Bishop Hooper.
The Holy Supper was " to be used as a communion unto
all men under both kinds, and not to be made a mass of
them that blasphemeth God ; for such as honour the
bread there for God, doth no less idolatry than they
that made the sun their God or stars."[3] The manner
in which this attitude is reflected in the notorious Black

Rubric and Article XXIX of the Forty-two Articles of 1553 is examined in detail in the final section of Chapter XII.

The Reformers' theories of precisely how Christ is present to the believer during the Lord's Supper are so varied and complex that it is not possible to discuss them in any detail here. The position is further complicated by frequent developments and modifications in their particular theories, " As to the nature of Cranmer's belief in the real presence of Our Lord in the Blessed Sacrament," complains Cardinal Gasquet, " it is always difficult to determine with precision, at any given time, the exact phase of a mind so shifting." The Cardinal claims, after studying the different theories in some detail, that the schools of opinion in the sixteenth century can be roughly classified into two categories— those who held the " real presence " and those who held the " real absence ".[4]

" The highest form—and yet far removed from the Catholic doctrine," writes Fr. Messenger, " was the theory of *Consubstantiation,* as put forward by Luther. The lowest form would be the symbolist view put forward by Zwingli, according to which the bread and wine merely ' represent' Christ's Body and Blood. Between these two extremes are all kinds of intermediate views, such as those of Bucer, Melancthon and Calvin, which may be described as *virtualistic views of the Presence.*"[5]   " Virtualism " is a term used to describe the belief according to which the *virtue* of Christ's Passion is received with the sacrament through faith. Bucer, who had more influence on Cranmer than any other Continental Reformer, totally rejected the Lutheran, let alone the Catholic, position that somehow Christ was received *in* or *under* the form of bread and wine. " He therefore proposed that the true statement of the matter should use the preposition *with.* The divine gift was not given *in* or *under* the forms of bread and wine—thus far Zwingli was right. But it was given in an indissoluble conjunction *with* them—as the bread is given to the body, so the divine gift passes into the faithful soul."[6]   It will be made clear during this chapter how faithfully Cranmer echoes this theory in his own explanations of the " real presence ". This fact is conceded by Anglican historians who have even gone as far as describing his views as "Zwinglio-Calvinistic ".[7] Zwingli and Calvin laid great stress on the fact that since the body and blood of Christ were not contained objectively in the sacrament they could not be offered by the priest. The concept of the Eucharistic oblation was, quite logically, bound up for them with what they continually denounced as " bread worship ".[8] This viewpoint is reproduced in Bishop Ridley's *Brief Declaration of the Lord's Supper*: " This kind of oblation standeth on transubstantiation, its german cousin, and do grow both upon one ground."[9] He agrees that if the Sacrament " be Christ's own natural body, born of the Virgin . . . then if the priest do offer the sacrament, he doth offer indeed Christ Himself." Francis Clark points out that: " this remark is another illustration of how the English Reformers understood their opponents' doctrine of the Mass."[10] He summarises the position of these English Reformers as follows: " As well as holding in common with all the Reformers the doctrine of salvation and faith that had dictated the original Lutheran rejection of the Mass, the leaders of the English Reformation shared with the Swiss divines an additional and compelling objection—that an oblation of Christ at the altar was in any case impossible because he was not objectively present there."[11]

Cranmer's views were certainly far nearer to those of Calvin and Zwingli than to those of Luther who " to the end of his life, believed that Christ is really present in what the communicant receives at the hand of the minister, and not only in the soul of the communicant as he receives. For Zwingli, what the communicant receives is bread and wine and no more than bread and wine."[12] This is a point which Cranmer never tired of stressing.

Bucer accepted that adoration must be a logical consequence of transubstantiation and the permanence of the Body and Blood of Christ under the species of bread and wine. He rejected these concepts " as the common

parents of impiety and superstition " and censured them
as a cause of superstition " inducing people to think
that, if any of the bread and wine of the communion
remain after it is over, there is something wrong in
applying it to common use as though there were in this
bread and wine in itself something divine or holy outside
of its use in communion."[13]   Bucer taught that: ". . .
the bread and wine are symbols of the body and blood
of Christ, by which He offers Himself to us. *But outside this use, they are what other bread and wine are.
For nothing of their nature is changed, and Christ the
Lord is not present in them,* but in the minds of the
faithful."[14]   It will be made clear how faithfully
Cranmer echoed this view.   The key-point which must
be borne in mind when discussing all the various shades
of *virtualism* or *receptionism* is that however realistic
the language used to describe Christ's Eucharistic
presence, it is a *spiritual* presence in the minds of the
faithful and not an *objective* presence in the consecrated
elements.   Cardinal Gasquet points out that: " The
' real presence ' is an ambiguous phrase and was
capable, as anyone acquainted with the polemical
writing of this period will acknowledge, of conveying, if
need be, the whole range of doctrine from that of the
Catholic Church to the congregations of Zurich and
Geneva."[15]   For this reason the term *substantial* rather
than *real* will be used here to convey the Catholic
teaching that Our Lord is present in the consecrated
elements by virtue of Transubstantiation, that after the
Consecration the bread and wine upon the altar become
" Christ's true Body which was born of the Virgin,
which hung on the Cross as an offering for the salvation
of the world and Which is seated at the right hand of
the Father, and Christ's true Blood Which flowed out
of His side ; they are such not simply because of the
Sacrament's symbolism and power but as constituted
by nature and as true substances."[16]

This chapter should make very clear the manner
in which the Reformers use Catholic terminology in a
sense that is a complete negation of Catholic belief.
The substantial presence of Christ in the Eucharist is

certainly a sacramental presence. Cranmer concedes that: "sacramentally and spiritually he *is* here present" but makes it quite clear that this means that He is *not* present substantially and that "Christ in his human nature is substantially, really, corporally, naturally, and sensibly present with his Father in Heaven . . ."—and nowhere else. "They (the papists) say," he writes, "that Christ is received in the mouth and entereth in with the bread and wine. We say that he is received in the heart and entereth in by faith."[17] This lucid rejection of Catholic teaching is made in a work in which Cranmer makes it quite clear that he fully grasps the Catholic standpoint and totally rejects it.

"Christ is present whensoever the Church prayeth unto him, and is gathered together in his name," he writes. "And the bread and wine be made unto us the Body and Blood of Christ (as it is in the book of Common Prayer), but *not* by changing the substance of the bread and wine into the substance of Christ's natural Body and Blood, but that in the *godly using of them they be unto the receivers* Christ's body and Blood . . . And therefore in the book of the holy communion *we do not pray absolutely* that the bread and wine may be made the Body and Blood of Christ, but *that unto us* in that holy mystery they may be so . . ."[18]

When Cranmer uses the term ' spiritually present' he means that Our Lord's Body, though Itself in heaven, is able, by Its innate power, to produce certain spiritual effects in the soul on earth which believes. He is very explicit about this in the preface to his treatise *On the Lord's Supper.*

"Moreover, when I say, and repeat many times in my book, that the body of Christ is present in them that worthily receive the sacrament; lest any man should mistake my words, and think that I mean, that although Christ be not corporally in the outward visible signs, yet he is corporally in the persons that duly receive them, this is to advertise the reader, that I mean no such thing; but my meaning is, that *the force, the grace, the virtue and benefit* of Christ's body that was crucified for us, and his Blood that was shed for us, be *really*

and effectually present with all them that duly receive
the sacraments: but all this I understand of his *spiritual*
presence, of which he saith, ' I will be with you unto
the world's end '; and ' wheresoever two or three be
gathered together in my name, there am I in the midst
of them '; and ' he that eateth my flesh and drinketh
my blood dwelleth in me and I in him '. Nor no more
truly is he corporally or really present in the due
ministration of the Lord's Supper, than he is in the due
ministration of baptism; that is to say, *in both
spiritually by grace.* And wheresoever in the scripture
it is said that Christ, God or the Holy Ghost is in any
man, the same is understood spiritually by grace."[19]

"Nothing could be more decisive than this," comment the English bishops in their *Vindication* of the Bull
Apostolicae Curae. " Being present spiritually, he tells
us, is being present by grace ; and being present by
grace means that the grace, not the Body, of Our Lord
is *really* present in the soul. That is what we Catholics
should ourselves say of the presence of Our Lord with
those gathered together in His name, or those undergoing Baptism. But a Presence in the Holy Eucharist
which is the same in kind as the Divine Presence in
Baptism is certainly not the Real Objective Presence
which the Church holds and professes."[20]

In this vindication, the Catholic bishops lay great
stress on Cranmer's explicit teaching that " evil men
receive not the Body and Blood in the Sacrament " and
the reason is that " they (the Body and Blood of Christ)
cannot be eaten and drunken but by spirit and faith
whereof ungodly men be destitute . . ."[21] He explains
that Christ's Body " cannot be eaten but spiritually by
believing and remembering Christ's benefits, and revolv-
ing them in our mind, believing that as the bread and
wine feed and nourish our bodies, so Christ feedeth
and nourisheth our souls."[22] Our bishops pointed out
that the faith to which Cranmer refers is that " illusory
feeling of assurance which is called ' justifying faith '
by the Lutherans and Calvinists ; for it is described
as a faith which the ungodly are incapable of having.

Hail, for mankind offered on the rood,*
For our redemption with thy blood made red,
Stung to the heart with a spear-head.
Now gracious Jesu, for thy wounds five,
Grant of they mercy before I be dead,
Clean housel** and shrift*** while I am alive."[30]

---

  * The Cross.
 ** Holy Communion.
*** Absolution.

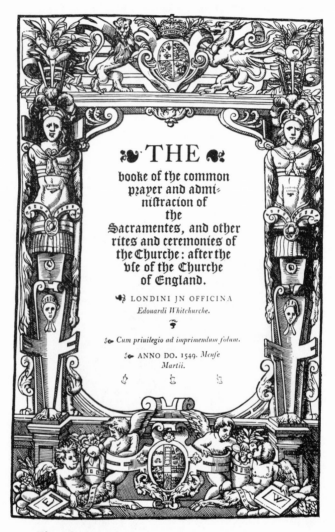

THE

booke of the common
prayer and admi-
nistracion of
the
Sacramentes, and other
rites and ceremonies of
the Churche: after the
use of the Churche
of England.

LONDINI JN OFFICINA
Edouardi Whitchurche.

Cum priuilegio ad imprimendum solum.

ANNO DO. 1549. *Mense
Martii.*

The title page of the 1549 Book of Common Prayer

Chapter VIII

LITURGICAL REVOLUTION

IT HAS already been demonstrated that the founders of the various Protestant heresies were revolutionaries rather than reformers. Their concern was not to reform the existing order but to introduce a new one. "The mania to ensure that all future history should date from their own reconstruction of primitive glory as they imagined this, characterized these revolutionaries as it has characterized all the rest, the social and political rebels as well as the religious . . . They were determined to destroy all that lay between themselves and the restoration of primitive Christianity as they conceived this to have been . . ."[1]

"In every community there are always many ready and eager for change, and many circumstances combined to make this the case during the short years of Edward's reign. The motives of a few, although they would seem to have been but a very few, were at least respectable, sincere and honest. Their reforming tendencies had been kept down for some years by the strong hand of Henry; but now these men found freedom to speak and hoped for freedom to act. The bulk however of the innovators were but an unruly mob, for whom destruction and freedom from restraint has ever been an attraction, and whose instinct is always against authority and tradition."[2]

"The most evident, not to say spectacular, changes were, of course, the alterations in the public services of religion. These were the changes which made the immediate—and generally hostile—impression on contemporaries; and it is these which have chiefly occupied the controversialists of our own time. But

even more important was the new basic theory of
religion which these changes presupposed and from
which they sprang."[3]

It has been shown in previous chapters that "the
new basic theory of religion", with the doctrine of
Justification by Faith alone as its basic axiom, was
radically incompatible with Catholic theology, particularly that of the Mass with its insistence on Transubstantiation and the Sacrifice of Christ's Body and Blood.
*"Accordingly, all the various schools of the Reformers
drew up new Communion rites."[4]* Dr. Brightman, the
noted Anglican liturgical historian, explains that
everything that signifies oblation is repudiated in the
four types of ritual produced by the Continental
Reformation from Wittenberg, Strassburg, and Geneva,
Zurich, and Cologne.[5] It will be shown that this was
also true of Cranmer's reforms which will be referred
to briefly in this chapter and treated in detail in Chapters
XI to XV.

A characteristic of the Protestant innovations is that
in both doctrine and liturgy they were imposed from
above by clerics backed by the support of those holding
civil power.[6] There was little enthusiasm for the
changes among the mass of the Faithful and sometimes
fierce opposition.[7] Commenting on the introduction of
Cranmer's first (1549) Prayer Book the Anglican Dean
of Bristol, Douglas Harrison, admits: "It is not surprising that it met with a reception which was nowhere
enthusiastic, and in the countryside there was violent
opposition both in East Anglia and in Devon and
Cornwall, where ten thousand 'stout and valiant per-
sonages' marched on Exeter demanding their old
services in Latin."[8]

In order not to over-alarm the Faithful, the first
Protestant Communion Services tended to be interim
measures, ambiguous rites which could pave the way
for more radical revisions to be introduced at a more
opportune moment. To assist in this purpose the basic
structure and many of the prayers of the Roman Mass
were retained where possible, sometimes even in Latin.

"To build up a new liturgy from the very foundation

was far from Luther's thoughts ... He preferred to make the best use of the Roman Mass, for one reason, as he so often insists, because of the weak, i.e. so as not to needlessly alienate the people from the new Church by the introduction of novelties. *From the ancient rite he merely eliminated all that had reference to the sacrificial character of the Mass. The Canon for instance, and the preceeding Offertory.* He also thought it best to retain the word ' Mass '."[9] Mgr. Hughes has this to say concerning the transformation of religious life in Saxony: " That the Mass must go because the Mass was a blasphemy was one certain first principle. But since, as Melanchthon said, ' the world is so much attached to the Mass that it seems impossible to wrest people from it ', Luther wished that the outward appearance of the service should be changed as little as possible. In this way the common people would never become aware there was any change, said Luther, and all would be accomplished ' without scandal '. ' There is no need to preach about this to the laity.' Even the communion was to be given under one species only to those who would otherwise cease to receive the Sacrament. Forms and appearances were comparatively unimportant, and in the later years Luther could say ' Thank God . . . our churches are so arranged that a layman, an Italian say, or a Spaniard, who cannot understand our preaching, seeing our Mass, choir, organs, bells etc. would surely say . . . there is no difference between it and his own."[10] Needless to say, although the other reformers began their revolutions with interim, ambiguous rites, the difference between their finalised services and the Mass would quickly have been apparent to any layman familiar with the former rite.

Like Luther, Cranmer included the word " Mass " in the description of his 1549 communion service: " The Supper of the Lorde and the Holy Communion, commonly called the Masse."[11]

The Spaniard, Francis Dryander, writing to the Zurich Protestants from Cambridge concerning this service remarked: " I think, however, that, by a resolution not

to be blamed, some puerilities have still been suffered
to remain, lest the people should be offended by too
great an innovation. These, trifling as they are, may
shortly be amended."[12] On the same ' puerilities ' Bucer
explains that these things ". . . are to be retained only
for a time, lest the people, not having learned Christ,
should be deterred by too extensive innovation from
embracing his religion."[13]

Dr. Darwell Stone writes that " it is probable that the
Prayer Book of 1549 represented rather what it was
thought safe to put out at the time than what Archbishop Cranmer and those who were acting with him
wished, and that at the time of the publication of the
book they already had in view a revision which would
approach much more nearly the position of the extreme
Reformers."[14] Canon E. C. Ratcliff makes the same
observation : " Its promoters regarded it as an interim
measure preparing the way for a more accurate embodi-
ment of their reforming opinions."[15] The general policy
of Cranmer and his friends was " to introduce the
Reformation by stages, gradually preparing men's minds
for more radical courses to come. At times compulsion
or intimidation was necessary in order to quell opposition, but their general policy was first to neutralise the
conservative mass of the people, to deprive them of
their Catholic-minded leaders, and then accustom them
by slow degrees to the new religious system. Cranmer
accordingly deplored the incautious zeal of men like
Hooper, which would needlessly provoke the conserva-
tives *and stiffen the attitude of that large class of men
who, rightly handled, could be brought to acquiesce in
ambiguity and interim measures.*"[16] Thus in England,
as in Germany, " in the first reformed liturgy, while
there was a resolute expunging of references to the
offering of Christ in the sacrament, much remained to
the scandal of the more uncompromising of the
Reformers."[17]

Many of the clergy " endeavoured to make the best
of an evil situation, and used the new communion
service as though it were the same as the ancient Mass,
which, of course, it was never intended to be."[18] This

happened to such an extent that Bucer complained:
" The Last Supper is in very many places celebrated as
the Mass, so much indeed that the people do not know
that it differs beyond that the vernacular tongue is
used."[19]

An accepted principle in regard to liturgical worship
is that the doctrinal standpoint of a Christian body
must necessarily be reflected in its worship. Liturgical
rites should express what they contain. It is not necessary for the Catholic position to be expressly contra-
dicted for a rite to become suspect ; the suppression
of prayers which had given liturgical expression to the
doctrine behind the rite is more than sufficient to give
cause for concern. This principle is embodied in the
phrase *legem credendi lex statuat supplicandi* ("let the
law of prayer fix the law of faith ")—in other words the
liturgy of the Church is a sure guide to her teaching.
This is usually presented in the abbreviated form of
lex orandi, lex credendi, and can be translated freely as
meaning that the manner in which the Church worships
(*lex orandi*) must reflect what the Church believes (*lex
credendi*). It would, of course, be a mistake to expect
to be able to deduce a system of doctrine from the
liturgical books of any Christian body and an attempt
to do this would be a misuse of the principle under
discussion here. A study of the liturgy is perhaps most
useful as a background to doctrinal belief—but where
changes, particularly omissions, are made, the doctrine
behind the revised liturgy becomes very much clearer.

When this principle is applied to the Protestant services, it reveals how clearly they embody the true
doctrinal position of the Reformers. " As in the new
communion service, so in the new ordination rite, *it
was not what was expressed but what was suppressed
that gave expression to the whole.*"[20] This factor was
considered of key importance by Pope Leo XIII when
he made the final decision on Anglican Orders—his
remarks concerning the Ordinal are equally applicable
to the changes in the Mass. " They (the Anglican
Reformers) knew only too well the intimate bond which
unites faith and worship, *lex credendi and lex suppli-*

candi: and so, under the pretext of restoring the order of the liturgy to its primitive form, they corrupted it in many respects to bring it into accord with the errors of the Innovators. As a result, not only is there in the whole Ordinal no clear mention of sacrifice, of consecration, of priesthood, of the power to consecrate and offer sacrifice, but, as We have already indicated, every trace of these and similar things remaining in such prayers of the Catholic rite as were not completely rejected, was purposely removed and obliterated."

Where the 1549 Prayer Book was concerned, it is not the fact that conservative-minded clergy such as Gardiner could use it "as though it were the same as the ancient Mass" which is important; it is the fact that it could be interpreted for what it was intended to be, for what the Continental Reformers intended their communion service to be, "*nothing else than a communion or synaxis*".[21] By a synaxis, they meant an assembly of the people gathered together under the presidency of the presiding minister to celebrate the memorial of the Lord in a commemorative supper where He would be present in the sense that He is always present where two or three are gathered together in His name. As Cranmer explained: "Christ is present whensoever the church prayeth unto Him, and is gathered together in His name. And the bread and wine be made unto us the body and blood of Christ (as it is in the book of common prayer), but not by changing the substance of the bread and wine into the natural substance of Christ's natural body and blood, but that in the godly using of them they be unto the receivers Christ's body and blood . . ."[22]

It has already been shown in Chapter VI that the Protestant use of the term "memorial" in no way corresponds to its use in Catholic theology.

The suppressions and additions which made the new communion services an accurate expression of Protestant theology, in complete conformity with the law *lex orandi, lex credendi,* were justified by the Reformers as being in accordance with, or a return to, primitive practice, a point made clear at the beginning of this chapter. The preamble to the Act of Uniformity claims that the compilers had " as well an eye and respect to the most sincere and pure Christian religion taught by the Scripture, as to the usages in the Primitive Church."[23] Fr. Messenger explains. " This of course merely means that, like all the Protestant Reformers, Cranmer aimed at a return to what he regarded as primitive purity and simplicity in contrast to the corruption and error of later Catholic times."[24] As for the mass of theological literature which had built up over the centuries and could not be reconciled with their new teachings—this they simply ignored.[25] " It is evident," wrote Luther, " that it is quite impossible for the Eucharist or Mass to be applied and communicated to another. What do I care, that the custom of the whole world holds otherwise and presumes to act accordingly?"[26]

A final principle of the Reformers was that there was no necessity for liturgical uniformity among the different churches. They maintained that a diversity of rite, traditions, ordinances and policies may exist among the churches. Such diversity " doth not dissolve and break the unity which is one God, one faith, one doctrine of Christ and His sacraments, preserved and kept in these several churches without any superiority or pre-eminence that one church by God's law may or ought to challenge over another."[27] As Cranmer made clear, once the Reformers were in a position to enforce their new services they were far more insistent upon the need for uniformity than the Catholic Church had ever been. Needless to say, the Catholic Church had never insisted on absolute liturgical uniformity—far from it. The various authorised rites within the Church were allowed to keep their own customs, rituals and liturgical languages without interference from Rome. Even within the Latin rite itself there was a degree of pluriformity in that there were differing usages, or in other words, not independent rites but variants of the Roman rites. The Dominican or Sarum Missals provide examples. As will be shown in Chapter X, *The Reform and the Missal of St. Pius V,* these usages within the

Latin rite did not differ from the Missal of St. Pius V on any important point.[28]   What the Reformers were trying to justify in their demand for pluriformity was the right to take an unprecedented step in the history of Christendom, the right to concoct new services. This in itself would have been a complete break with tradition—up to this point the liturgy had developed by a process of natural evolution. Some ceremonies and prayers were gradually discarded as the centuries passed, for example the Bidding Prayers or the practice of having two lessons before the Gospel. Others were added, such as the Last Gospel. Any attempt to bring about a clear break with any traditional usage should automatically arouse the suspicions of the orthodox, even if ostensibly plausible motives are adduced for doing so. This point will be developed in Chapter IX: *The Principles of Liturgical Reform.* In this case, the new services were a blatant attempt to express the beliefs of a new religion.

Reference has already been made to the Bull *Apostolicae Curae* in which Pope Leo XIII decided irrevocably that Anglican Orders are invalid.[29] In an attempt to refute the Bull, the Anglican Archbishops issued an official reply. This was answered by Cardinal Vaughan and his fellow Bishops of the Province of Westminster in a book entitled *A Vindication of the Bull Apostolicae Curae.* Like Pope Leo, the Catholic Bishops lay great stress on the question of omissions, not simply as regards the Ordinal but also in the Communion service. " To put the matter briefly, if the First Prayer Book of Edward VI is compared with the Missal, sixteen omissions can be detected of which the evident purpose was to eliminate the idea of sacrifice. Moreover, whereas even after that drastic treatment there still remained a few phrases and rubrics on which Gardiner could fasten, endeavouring to understand them as still asserting the Real Objective Eucharistic Presence and the True Sacrifice, all these phrases and rubrics were altered in the revised Prayer Book of 1552."[30]

The Anglican claims that their services aimed at

simplicity and a return to primitive usage were dealt with in very vigorous language. The Catholic Bishops deny the right of national or local churches to *devise* their own rites. " They must not omit or reform anything in those forms which immemorial tradition has bequeathed to us. For such an immemorial usage, whether or not it has in the course of ages incorporated superfluous accretions, must, in the estimation of those who believe in a divinely guarded visible Church, at least have retained whatever is necessary ; so that in adhering rigidly to the rite handed down to us we can always feel secure ; whereas, if we omit or change anything, we may perhaps be abandoning just that element which is essential. And this sound method is that which the Catholic Church has always followed . . . That in earlier times local churches were permitted to *add* new prayers and ceremonies is acknowledged . . . But that they were permitted to *subtract* prayers and ceremonies in previous use, and even to remodel the existing rites in the most drastic manner, is a proposition for which we know of no historical foundation, and which appears to us absolutely incredible. Hence Cranmer, in taking this unprecedented course, acted, in our opinion, with the most inconceivable rashness."[31]

The detailed comparison between the Missal and the 1549 Prayer Book suggested by the Catholic Bishops will be undertaken in Chapter XII. It could be argued that since this Missal (that of St. Pius V) was not promulgated until 1570 it is hardly fair to compare it with a Communion service published in 1549. This point has already been dealt with in Note 28 to this chapter but will be studied in detail in Chapter X: *The Reform and the Missal of St. Pius V*. A study of this reform will also demonstrate the manner in which the principles governing liturgical development which have been quoted from the Catholic Bishops' *Vindication* were observed meticulously by this great saint and totally violated by the Protestant Reformers. Before doing this, a more detailed examination of these principles will be made in the next chapter.

PIVS EPISCOPVS

SERVVS SERVORVM DEI,

Ad perpetuam rei memoriam.

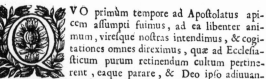 VO primùm tempore ad Apoſtolatus api-
cem aſſumpti fuimus, ad ea libenter ani-
mum, vireſque noſtras intendimus, & cogi-
tationes omnes direximus, quæ ad Eccleſia-
ſticum purum retinendum cultum pertine-
rent, eaque parare, & Deo ipſo adiuuan-
te, omni adhibito ſtudio efficere contendimus. Cúmque
inter alia ſacri Tridentini Concilij decreta, nobis ſtatuendum
eſſet de ſacris libris, Catechiſmo, Miſſali, & Breuiario edendis
atque emendandis: edito iam, Deo ipſo annuente, ad populi
eruditionem Catechiſmo, & ad debitas Deo perſoluendas lau-
des Breuiario cáſtigato, omnino vt Breuiario Miſſale reſpon-
deret, vti congruum eſt, & conueniens (cùm vnum in Eccleſia
Dei pſallendi modum, vnum Miſſæ celebrandæ ritum eſſe
maximè deceat) neceſſe iam videbatur, vt quod reliquum in
hac parte eſſet, de ipſo nempe Miſſali edendo, quàm primùm
cogitaremus. Quare eruditis delectis viris onus hoc demandan-
dum duximus: qui quidem diligenter collatis omnibus cum ve-
tuſtis noſtræ Vaticanæ Bibliothecæ, aliiſque vndique conquiſi-
tis, emendatis atque incorruptis codicibus, necnon veterum
conſultis ac probatorum auctorum ſcriptis, qui de ſacro eorum-
dem rituum inſtituto monumenta nobis reliquerunt, ad pri-
ſtinam Miſſale ipſum ſanctorum Patrum normam ac ritum re-
ſtituerunt. Quod recognitum iam & caſtigatum, maturè adhi-
bita conſideratione, vt ex hoc inſtituto, cœptoque labore fru-
ctus omnes percipiant, Romæ quàm primùm imprimi, atque
impreſſum edi mandauimus: nempe, vt ſacerdotes intelligant,
quibus precibus vti, quos ritus quaſue cæremonias in Miſſa-
rum celebratione retinere poſt hac debeant. Vt autem à ſacro-
ſancta Romana Eccleſia, cæterarum Eccleſiarũ matre & magiſtra

A ij

Quo Primum: the opening page of the Bull

Chapter IX

THE PRINCIPLES OF LITURGICAL REFORM

"We never disparage the faith of our fathers but hand it on exactly as we have received it. God willed that the truth should come down to us from pastor to pastor, from hand to hand, without any evident novelties. It is in this way that we recognise what has always been believed and, accordingly, what must always be believed. It is, so to speak, from this word **always** that the truth and the promise derive their authority, an authority which would vanish completely the moment an interruption was discovered anywhere."—Bossuet: Pastoral Letter to the new Catholics of his diocese.

" THE FORMS of public prayers are the very centre and kernel of the religious life of a Christian people," wrote Cardinal Gasquet.[1] This is a fact of which the Catholic Church has always been keenly aware and her liturgical traditions have been regarded as a sacred trust. Even " what we may call the ' archaisms ' of the Missal are the expression of the faith of our fathers which it is our duty to watch over and hand on to posterity," explained Dom Cabrol, ' father ' of the liturgical movement.[2] When St. Pius X wrote his Encyclical *Pascendi Dominici Gregis,* exposing the doctrines and methods of the modernists, he found it necessary to repeat the condemnation of the Council of Nicea aimed at those " who dare, after the impious fashion of heretics, to invent novelties of some kind . . . or endeavour by malice or craft to overthrow any one of the legitimate traditions of the Catholic Church ".[3]

The soundest principle for any liturgical reformer to use as the basis for his plan to revise the liturgy is " Don't!" This is the traditional principle upon which

the Catholic Church in east and west has based her
attitude to changes in the outward forms of public
worship—and where the laity are concerned this can,
for practical purposes, be narrowed down to the celebration of Mass. The principles to be discussed in this
chapter are less applicable to such matters as the
Breviary. The sentiments expressed by Bossuet are
echoed in an exceptionally profound analysis of the
sociological implications of liturgical reform written in
1974 by Professor James Hitchcock. He formulates as
a principle that: "Catholicism, although open to
change, manifests a decided bias toward stability and
toward the preservation of the past. This is because one
of its principal tasks in the world is to witness to the
reality of eternity ; hence it cultivates what is timeless,
enduring, and stable to serve as hints of eternity."[4]

Cardinal Gasquet rightly remarks that any Catholic
who sees in the living Liturgy of the Roman Church
essential forms which remain what they were as much
as 1,400 years ago cannot "but feel a personal love for
those sacred rites when they come to him with all the
authority of centuries. Any rude handling of such
forms must cause deep pain to those who know and
use them. For they come to them from God, through
Christ and through the Church. But they would not
have such an attraction were they not also sanctified
by the piety of so many generations who have prayed
in the same words and found in them steadiness in joy
and consolation in sorrow."[5]

Liturgical laws, although coming within the category
of ecclesiastical law, must be governed by the same
principles by which any human law can be judged. The
prayers in the Mass and the rubrics governing its celebration are generally the codification of practices
already established by custom. "Liturgies are not made,
they grow in the devotion of centuries" notes Professor
Owen Chadwick in his history of the Reformation.[6]

Only heretics ever attempted any radical reform of
the Liturgy. Nor were the basic prayers, gestures and
rubrics from which the various rites grew the creation
of committees and commissions set up to devise litur-

gical forms. It would be impossible to find evidence of
some form of liturgical commission being set up in the
early Church which decided, for example, that it would
be fitting for the priest to kiss the altar from time to
time, deciding upon the most appropriate moments for
this to be done, and then composing rubrics to ensure
that priests acted upon their instructions in future.
What happened was that the priest kissed the altar at
certain times as a result of customs which had grown
up naturally, and eventually this gesture was formally
codified as a rubric. The genuflection at the *Incarnatus*
in both the Creed and the Last Gospel both began as
acts of popular faith in and devotion to the Incarnation,
which is the basis of our entire faith. These genuflec-
tions had become general customs long before they
were codified as rubrics. Hugh Ross Williamson explains that: " One of the Church's replies to the menace
of Catharism was the institution in 1285 of the recita-
tion by the priest on his way back from the altar to the
sacristy of the Last Gospel. His genuflection at ' the
Word was made flesh ' was the guarantee that he was
not a secret Cathar and that in the Mass he had just
celebrated his intention was to effect Transubstantiation."[7] It is interesting to note that this custom found
its way into liturgies as varied as the Roman and Sarum
rites. Similarly, the elevation and adoration of the
consecrated Host was a popular reaction by both clergy
and people against the denial of the Real Presence.
The ringing of a bell at certain points in the Mass had
the practical purpose of making those unable to see the
altar aware of the most significant moments in the
Mass. St. Thomas Aquinas assures us that the Holy
Ghost protects the Church from error in the development of liturgical customs and laws.[8]

An examination of any form of human law—common
law, liturgical law, laws relating to games, or the laws
of grammar—makes it clear that they have no intrinsic
value in themselves but are simply a means to an end
—and that end is the common good of those for whom
they are ordained. There is no intrinsic merit in driving on the left side of the road or on the right—but it

is clearly in the common interests of all motorists that in any particular country they should all drive on the same side.

St. Thomas defines a law as " An ordinance governed by reason promulgated for the common good by the person having authority within a community." The consensus of Catholic authorities agrees with St. Thomas in his exposition of the nature of human law, namely, that whether civil or ecclesiastical it is an act of public authority having the right to demand obedience but which itself must conform to the demands of reason and to be seen to have an effect that is both good and to the benefit of those for whom it is intended.[9]

St. Thomas, followed by other authorities, warns that any change in existing legislation must be made only with extreme caution, particularly where it might involve changes in any long-standing customs. He treats the question of the mutation of laws in his *Summa Theologica*. In discussing the question of the mutation of laws he lays down the premise that there are two remote reasons which can lead to a just change in the laws.[10] The first resides in the nature of man who, being a rational being, is gradually led by his reason from what is less perfect to what is more perfect. The second reason must be found in the actions which are being subjected to the regulation of law and which can change according to the various circumstances in which men find themselves and in which they must work. Every change in law *must* be determined by an *evident necessity* of the common good since law is rightly changed only insofar as this change manifestly contributes to the welfare of the community. " It is well known," writes Louis Salleron, " that a tried and tested revolutionary technique for overthrowing established societies is the call for a return to its origins. It is no longer a question of pruning the tree so that it will bear better fruit ; it must be sawn down at its very base under the pretext of reinvigorating the roots."[11]

Pascal notes that custom is the whole of equity for the sole reason that it is accepted and that anyone who tries to trace it back to its first principles will destroy

it. "The art of opposition and rebellion lies in under-
mining established customs by tracing them back to
their origins in order to reveal their lack of authority
and justice. 'We must,' it is said, 'go back to the
primitive and fundamental laws of the State which
have been abolished by unjust custom.' It is the surest
way of losing everything; nothing will appear just
when subjected to a test of that kind."[12]

Even where a change in the law carries some obvious
benefit it will be accompanied by some harm to the
common good as any change in the law abandons a
custom, and custom is always a great help and support
in the observance of laws. Any change in an individual
law diminishes the force and respect paid to Law
because a custom is taken away. St. Thomas, with
profound psychological insight, adds that this is true
even when the innovations contrary to custom are minor
ones, for, even though minor in themselves, they may
appear important in the common estimation. From this
he draws a general conclusion; law must never be
changed unless it is *certain* that the common good will
find in the modification at least an adequate compensa-
tion for the harm by way of derogating a custom. A
principle enunciated by Professor Hitchcock is that:
"The decline of a sense of tradition in the Church
severely weakens not only its continuity with the ages
past but also its coherence in the present age."[13]
Professor Johannes Wagner, Director of the Liturgical
Institute of Treves, reached the same conclusion when
he stated: "History has proved a thousand times that
there is nothing more dangerous for a religion, nothing
is more likely to result in discontent, incertitude, divi-
sion, and apostasy than interference with the liturgy
and consequently with religious sensibility."[14]

Suarez, another great authority, insists that for his
law to be considered reasonable, a legislator must not
simply refrain from demanding something his subjects
will find impossible to carry out, but the law must not
even be too difficult, distressing or disagreeable, taking
account of human frailty. On no account should it
contradict any reasonable custom because custom is a

kind of "second nature" and what it finds abhorrent
"is considered to be morally impossible." He also lays
great stress on the necessity for laws to be permanent—
not in the sense that they can never be abrogated but
that this shall only occur if changing circumstances
make it quite clear that they are no longer just. If it
is to work in the common interest legislation must aim
at stability and uniformity within the community.[15]
Where there is the least doubt that the benefits of a
change in the laws are likely to outweigh considerably
the harm that will result in a change of custom then it
is better to conserve the existing legislation rather than
change it. Being the accepted practice, it has, so to
speak, the right of possession and, in a case of doubt,
it is the right of possession which is the stronger.

Another principle stated by Professor Hitchcock is
that: "The manipulation of sacred symbols to give
increased meaning to the liturgy tends instead to
destroy its meaning and alienate the participants from
the Church's worship."[16]

In his Apostolic Constitution *Auctorem Fidei* (28
August, 1794) Pope Pius VI condemned the pseudo-
Synod of Pistoia for its desire to return to what it
claimed were more primitive sources by simplifying the
rites, using the vernacular, and saying the entire Mass
in an audible tone. The Pope laid particular stress on
the fact that this Synod had suggested a conflict between the principles which should govern the celebration of the Liturgy and the order *currently in use,*
accepted and approved by the Church. The proposed
changes were condemned as "*false, disturbing the
prescribed order of the celebration of the mysteries,*
and easily productive of many evils." The history of
the various Christian denominations is replete with
instances of disruption and even schisms concerning
changes in established customs, changes which many
modern commentators might regard as trivial matters.
The secession of the Old Believers from the Russian
Orthodox Church is a typical example. What such inci-
dents do prove is the accuracy of St. Thomas's insight
into the harmful effects of changing the status quo

without overwhelming reasons for doing so. Professor Hitchcock states that: " The rejection of traditional ritual places the individual outside his community and is hence an alienating experience ; it tends not toward an increase of happiness or meaning but the reverse."[17]

Such is the reverence of the Catholic Church for legitimate traditions that where a custom can be shown to have been observed continuously for a period as short as forty years it is given the force of law in the Canon Law of the Church, even if it has never been expressly codified. Such a custom can only be abro- gated by legislation expressly formulated to do so, and where any doubt exists the more recent law must be considered in relation to the older one and, as far as possible, reconciled with it ; in other words, where doubt exists the existing law can continue to be observed. Even where new legislation contains a nonobstant clause expressly prohibiting any contrary law or custom, this prohibition cannot extend to custom of a hundred years or immemorial standing unless the new law refers to them explicitly.

The testimony of the great Catholic Doctors is re- inforced by the opinion of Rousseau, who could hardly be described as sympathetic to the Church ! " It is above all the great antiquity of laws which renders them holy and venerable ; people soon despise those which they see constantly changing."[18] " Sacred rituals," observes Professor Hitchcock, " cannot be reformed substantially without serious dislocation in the society whose symbols they are."[19]

The application of these principles to the liturgical changes of the Protestant Reformation is best illustrated by quoting again from the statement of the Catholic Bishops of England and Wales in support of *Apostolicae Curae,* already quoted at the conclusion of Chapter VIII. Referring to Cranmer's reforms, our Bishops insist that local churches are not entitled to devise new rites. " They must not omit or reform anything in those forms which immemorial tradition has bequeathed to us. For such an immemorial usage, whether or not it has in the course of ages incorporated superfluous accretions, must, in the estimation of those who believe in a divinely guarded, visible Church, at least have retained whatever is necessary; so that in adhering rigidly to the rite handed down to us we can always feel secure: whereas if we omit or change anything, we may perhaps be abandoning just that element which is essential . . . that they were permitted to subtract prayers and ceremonies in previous use, and even to remodel the existing rites in a most drastic manner, is a proposition for which we know of no historical foundation, and which appears to us absolutely incredible."[20]

The effects upon the religious life of Britain of the Protestant reforms is only one of many examples, which prove the truth of Confucius' dictum that " to interfere with the public rites is to interfere with the very fabric of government." This does not, of course, preclude any liturgical reform—but a reform need not necessitate drastic remodelling of existing rites ; to do this is rather to perpetrate a liturgical revolution of the type described in Chapter VIII. The total incompatibility of any radical reform of the Catholic liturgy with the ethos and traditions of the Church is well expressed by Professor Hitchcock: " The radical and deliberate alteration of ritual leads inevitably to the radical alteration of belief as well.

" This radical alteration causes an immediate loss of contact with the living past of the community, which comes instead to be a deadening burden.

" The desire to shed the burden of the past is incompatible with Catholicism, which accepts history as an organic development from ancient roots and expresses this acceptance in a deep respect for Tradition."[21]

It is quite possible to reform the liturgy in accordance with the principles enunciated in this chapter, principles based not simply on the teaching of the great Catholic Doctors but on the common wisdom of mankind. Such a reform was enacted by St. Pius V with the promulgation of the Bull *Quo Primum* in 1570. Before examining this reform in detail it might be well to comment on a remark made by a character in Tolstoy's *Anna Karenina:* " Supposing you wanted to lay out a garden in front of

your house, and on the very spot there was a tree that's
stood there for centuries. However old and gnarled,
you would not cut it down to make room for flower-
beds, would you? You would plan your flower-beds
round the old tree. You couldn't grow a tree like that
in a year."[22]

Perhaps the most simple criterion for distinguishing
between a liturgical reformer such as Pope St. Pius V,
and a revolutionary such as Thomas Cranmer, is that
the latter would take his axe with the greatest gusto to
any tree standing in his path, however old and however
gnarled!

MISSALE

ROMANVM,

Ex Decreto Sacro-sancti Concilij Tridentini restitutum.

Pii V. Pont. Max. iussu editum,
E T
Clementis VIII. auctoritate recognitum.

In quo Missæ de SANCTIS omnes ad longum recèns positæ sunt, pro faciliori Celebrantium commoditate.

Vnà cum Missis omnium Nouorum Sanctorum, ab VRBANO VIII. concessis.

LVTETIÆ PARISIORVM,

Apud { Viduam Sebastiani Hvrè', E T Sebastianvm Hvrè'. } viâ Iacobæâ sub signo Cordis-boni.

M. DC. LII.

Missale Romanum: *the title page of the French edition of 1652*

Chapter X

THE REFORM AND THE MISSAL OF ST. PIUS V

" The most beautiful thing this side of heaven."
—Father Faber.

" UNIFORMITY IN Liturgy throughout the Church has never been a Catholic ideal. No one wants to replace the Eastern Liturgies, or even those of Milan and Toledo, by that of Rome. But it is a reasonable ideal that those who use the Roman rite should use it uniformly in a pure form."[1] At the time of the Council of Trent there was a great deal of variety in local usage. A proliferation of local rites had evolved during the Middle Ages, such as the Sarum rite in England. These were merely variations of the Roman rite and must not be confused with such important traditions as the Mozarabic or Ambrosian liturgies which can justly be regarded as separate rites. Father Fortescue explains that:
" In everything of any importance at all, Sarum (and all the other medieval rites) was simply Roman, the rite which we still use. Not only was the whole order and arrangement the same, all the important elements were the same too. The essential element, the Canon, was word for word the same as ours. No medieval bishop dared to touch the sacred Eucharistic prayer."[2] The Protestant Reformation provided a stimulus to the need for some degree of liturgical reform which, in any case, would have been necessary.
" The Protestant Reformers naturally played havoc with the old Liturgy. It was throughout the expression of the very ideas (the Real Presence, Eucharistic Sacrifice and so on) they rejected. So they substituted for

it new communion services that expressed their principle but, of course, broke away utterly from all historic
liturgical evolution.   The Council of Trent (1545-1563),
in opposition to the anarchy of these new services,
wished the Roman Mass to be celebrated uniformly
everywhere.   The medieval local uses had lasted long
enough.   They had become very florid and exuberant ;
and their variety caused confusion."[3]

In its eighteenth session the Council appointed a
commission to examine the Missal, to revise it and to
restore it " according to the custom and rite of the Holy
Fathers ", using for that purpose the best manuscripts
and other documents.   " They accomplished their task
very well," comments Father Fortescue.   " On 14th July,
1570, the Pope published the reformed Missal by the
Bull *Quo Primum,* still printed at the beginning.   Its
title was: *Missale Romanum ex decreto ss. Concilii
Tridentini restitutum.*"[4]   St. Pius is honoured by the
Church as an instrument chosen by God *ad conterendos
Ecclesiae hostes et ad divinum cultum reparandum.*

This reform was carried out wholly in accordance
with the principles enunciated in Chapter IX.   Nothing
could have been a greater contrast to the *revolution*
described in Chapter VIII.   Up to the time of St. Pius
V the history of the Roman rite had been one of natural
and gradual development.   Father David Knowles,
Britain's most distinguished Catholic scholar until his
death in 1974, explained that: " The Missal of 1570
was indeed the result of instructions given at Trent,
but it was, in fact, as regards the Ordinary, Canon,
Proper of the time and much else a replica of the Roman
Missal of 1474, which in its turn repeated in all essentials the practice of the Roman Church of the epoch of
Innocent III, which itself derived from the usage of
Gregory the Great and his successors in the seventh
century.   In short, the Missal of 1570 was in essentials
the usage of the mainstream of medieval European
Liturgy which included England and its rites."[5]

Fr. Fortescue considers that the reign of St. Gregory
the Great marks an epoch in the history of the Mass,
having left the liturgy in its essentials just as we have

it today. There is, moreover, a constant tradition that St. Gregory was the last to touch the essential part of the Mass, namely the Canon. Benedict XIV (1740-1758) says: "No Pope has added to or changed the Canon since St. Gregory."[6] Whether this is totally accurate is not a matter of great importance; even if some very minor additions did creep in afterwards, perhaps a few Amens, the important point is that a tradition of more than a millenium certainly existed in the Roman Church that the Canon should not be changed. "This fact, that it has so remained unaltered during thirteen centuries, is the most speaking witness of the veneration with which it has always been regarded and of the scruple which has ever been felt at touching so sacred a heritage, coming to us from unknown antiquity."[7]

Although the rite continued to develop after the time of St. Gregory: "All later modifications were fitted into the old arrangement, and the most important parts were not touched. From, roughly, the time of St. Gregory we have the text of the Mass, its order and arrangement, as a sacred tradition that no one has ventured to touch except in unimportant details."[8]

Among these additions: "The prayers said at the foot of the altar are in their present form the latest part of all. They developed out of medieval private preparations and were not formally appointed in their present state before the Missal of Pius V (1570)."[9] They were, however, widely used well before the Reformation as is proved by the fact that both Luther and Cranmer considered it necessary to abolish the *Judica me,* with its reference to the priest going to the altar of God, and the *Confiteor*—as will be shown in Chapter XII where Cranmer's 1549 Communion service is studied in detail.

"The *Gloria* was introduced gradually, at first only to be sung on feasts and at bishop's Masses. It is probably Gallican. The Creed came to Rome in the XIth century. The Offertory prayers and the *Lavabo* were introduced from beyond the Alps hardly before the XIVth century. The *Placeat,* Blessing and the Last

Gospel were introduced gradually in the Middle Ages."[10]

It should be pointed out that these prayers almost invariably have a liturgical use stretching back centuries before their official incorporation into the Roman rite. The *Suscipe Sancte Pater* can be traced back to the prayer book of Charles the Bald (875-877).[11] It would be a serious mistake to conclude with regard to the Roman or any other liturgy that an older form must be better. It is not surprising that as the Roman rite spread throughout the West in the sixth, seventh, and eighth centuries, gradually supplanting the existing rites, it was also influenced by them. The fusion of the original Roman rite with various Gallican elements explains the emergence of the various medieval derived rites, not really rites at all but simply variations of the Roman rite. The Canon, of course, remained unchanged. Had the Roman rite been totally satisfactory, satisfying both to priests and people, it is unlikely that elements incorporated from the Gallican rites would have eventually found their way into the liturgy at Rome itself. This is a form of liturgical development totally in accord with the principles enunciated in Chapter IX. It will also be noticed when reading Chapter XII that the prayers which came into the Roman Mass after the time of Gregory the Great were among the first to be discarded by the Reformers—this is hardly surprising as one of the reasons which must have prompted the Church to accept them, guided by the Holy Ghost, is the exceptional clarity of their doctrinal content. This tendency for a rite to express ever more clearly what it contains is in perfect accord with the principle *lex orandi, lex credendi*.

In the authoritative exposition of Catholic doctrine edited by Canon George Smith it is stated that: ". . . throughout the history of the development of the sacramental liturgy, the tendency has always been towards growth—additions and accretions, the effort to obtain a fuller, more perfect, more clearly significant symbolism."[12] This is fully in accord with Cardinal Newman's third characteristic of a true development—the power of assimilation. " In the physical world, whatever has life is characterised by growth, so that in no respect to grow is to cease to live. It grows by taking into its own substance external materials ; and this absorption or assimilation is completed when the materials appropriated come to belong to it or enter into its unity . . . An eclectic, conservative, assimilating, healing, moulding process, a unitive power, is of the essence, and a third test, of a faithful development."[13]

These additions did not only enrich the Mass doctrinally. "If one may venture a criticism of these additions from an aesthetic point of view," writes Fr. Fortescue, "it is that they are exceedingly happy. The Old Roman Rite, in spite of its dignity and archaic simplicity, had the disadvantage of being dull. The Eastern and Gallican liturgies are too florid for our taste and too long. The few non-Roman elements in our Mass take nothing from its dignity and yet give it enough variety and reticent emotion to make it beautiful."[14]

It should already be quite clear what a radical difference there was between the type of reform enacted by St. Pius V and the "unprecedented" action of the Protestant Reformers in devising "their own rites", so vigorously and so justly condemned by the Catholic Hierarchy of England and Wales in the passage cited at the conclusion of Chapters VIII and IX. The nature of the reform of St. Pius V can best be expressed by citing Fr. Fortescue in regard to a part of the Mass that has already been mentioned—the prayers at the foot of the altar.

" A confession of sins is also a preparation common to most rites. It was the Missal of Pius V that finally fixed the celebrant's prayers in the form we know. They had long existed in this or similar combinations, together with alternative sets of prayers. The revisers of the Tridentine commission only adopted uniformity in the use of one of the most widespread forms."[15] Contrast this with the methods adopted by Cranmer which are discussed in Chapter XI.

Commenting on the Bull *Quo Primum,* Fr. Raymond Dulac remarks that : " It is characteristic of a truly

great leader that the more firm he is in imposing obliga-
tions the more scrupulous will he be in respecting rights ;
not simply the general and absolute rights of the
abstract ' person ', but the historic rights of individuals
and particular communities, even when acquired solely
by custom."[16] Pope St. Pius V permitted the retention
of any rite that could show a prescription of two centuries as well as those of such religious orders as the
Dominicans, Carmelites, and Carthusians. " After con-
firming the right of religious orders, chapters, etc. to
the peaceful possession of their missals," writes Fr.
Dulac, " Pius V permits such communities to renounce
them in favour of his own, *si iisdem magis placeret*: if
his own missal pleases them more. But on one condition, that this preference is approved by their Bishop
or Superior as well as by ' the whole chapter '." Here
again, the Pope, while favouring his own Missal, in
certain cases does not wish to infringe established rights,
and indeed, allows them priority. In this respect we
must bear in mind that these particular Missals are
fundamentally identical with the Roman one presenting
purely minor variations. It is worth noting that the
Mass brought to England and Wales by the martyr
priests in the reign of Elizabeth I was, in fact, that of
St. Pius V. It was adopted by the English College at
Douay and George Godsalf, ordained on 20th December,
1576, must have been the first English priest to offer
Mass according to the reformed Missal.[17]

There have been revisions since the reform of St.
Pius V but, as Fr. Fortescue explains, up to his time
(1917) these had been intended to keep the Missal in
line with the reform of 1570. " By the time of Clement
VIII (1592-1605) printers had corrupted the text in
several ways." The work of the commission appointed
by Clement VIII " was only to correct these corrup-
tions. They did not in any way modify the Mass . . .
Benedict XIV (1740-1758), who did so much for the
reform of the liturgy did not revise the Missal."[18] Fr.
Fortescue deals with all the subsequent revisions up to
his time in detail and concludes that: " Since the
Council of Trent the history of the Mass is hardly any-

thing but the composition and approval of new Masses.
The scheme and all the fundamental parts remain the
same. No one has thought of touching the venerable
liturgy of the Roman Mass, except by adding to it new
Propers."[19]

The Reforms of Pius XII did go farther than this,
notably in regard to the Holy Week services. But any
objective assessment of his reforms will find them totally
in accord with the principles laid down in Chapter IX
and, needless to say, the Mass itself was not changed in
any way.

" Essentially the Missal of St. Pius V is the Gregorian
Sacramentary," writes Fr. Fortescue, " that again is
formed from the Gelasian book which depends on the
Leonine collection. We find the prayers of our Canon
in the treatise *de Sacramentis* and allusions to it in the
IVth century. So our Mass goes back without essential
change, to the age when it first developed out of the
oldest liturgy of all. It is still redolent of that liturgy,
of the days when Caesar ruled the world and thought
he could stamp out the Faith of Christ, when our fathers
met together before dawn and sang a hymn to Christ
as God. The final result of our enquiry is that, in spite
of unsolved problems, in spite of later changes, there
is not in Christendom another rite so venerable as
ours."[20]

And again:

" The Missal of Pius V is the one we still use. Later
revisions are of slight importance. No doubt in every
reform one may find something that one would have
preferred not to change. Still, a just and reasonable
criticism will admit that Pius V's restoration was on the
whole eminently satisfactory. The standard of the
commission was antiquity. They abolished later ornate
features and made for simplicity, yet without destroying all those picturesque elements that add poetic
beauty to the severe Roman Mass. They expelled the
host of long sequences that crowded the Mass continually, but kept what are undoubtedly the five best ;
they reduced processions and elaborate ceremonials, yet
kept the really pregnant ceremonies, candles, ashes,

palms, and the beautiful Holy Week rites. Certainly we
in the West must be very glad that we have the Roman
rite in the form of Pius V's missal . . . There are many
days on which we say the Mass that has been said for
centuries, back to the days of the Gelasian and Leonine
book. And when they do come, the new Masses only
affect the Proper. Our Canon is untouched, and all the
scheme of the Mass. Our Missal is still that of Pius V.
We may be very thankful that his Commission was so
scrupulous to keep or restore the old Roman tradition."[21]

The antiquity of the Roman Mass is a point which
needs to be stressed. There is what Fr. Fortescue
describes as a " prejudice that imagines that everything
Eastern must be old." This is a mistake and there is
no existing Eastern liturgy with a history of continual
use stretching back as far as that of the Roman Mass.[22]
This is particularly true with regard to the Roman
Canon. Dom Cabrol, O.S.B., " father " of the modern
liturgical movement, stresses that " The Canon of our
Roman Rite, which in its main lines was drawn up in
the fourth century, is the oldest and most venerable
example of all the Eucharistic prayers in use today."[23]
In a similar vein, Fr. Louis Bouyer, one of the leaders
of the modern liturgical movement up to the time of
Vatican II, stresses that: " The Roman Canon, as it is
today, goes back to Gregory the Great. There is not,
in the East or West, a Eucharistic prayer, remaining in
use to this day, that can boast such antiquity. In the
eyes not only of the Orthodox but of Anglicans and
even those Protestants who have still, to some extent,
a feeling for tradition, to jettison it would amount to a
rejection of any claim on the part of the Roman
Church, to represent the true Catholic Church."[24]

It is scarcely possible to exaggerate the importance of
the Roman Missal from any standpoint. At a time when
everything in contemporary society seemed to be
changing, the fact that, up to 1964 a sacrifice in a form
and language stretching back over fifteen centuries was
still offered daily in this nuclear age in churches and
cathedrals from Bosnia to Boston, from the Hebrides to
Tokyo, provided—religious considerations apart—a

unique if not miraculous cultural survival. Even an
unbeliever with the least vestige of imagination could
not have failed to be moved when travelling across
Europe by train if he realized that an awesome sacrifice was offered daily with identical gestures, using the
same sacral language, in the innumerable churches,
abbeys, and cathedrals whose spires, domes, and turrets
dominated every hamlet, village, town and city through
which his train passed, no matter what the country or
what the language. The essential unity of Catholics in
these different countries derived from their member-
ship of the same Church and their possession of the
same sacraments and sacrifice—but in the Latin rite
this unity was deepened and made manifest by their
common use of the Missal of St. Pius V, the Pope
chosen by God *ad contenderos Ecclesiae hostes ad
divinum cultum reparandum.* The impression these
facts made upon a believer is incalculably greater. A
Catholic knows that the most vital moment in human
history took place outside Jerusalem nearly 2,000 years
ago when a mother stood weeping by a cross upon which
her torn and broken Son offered His life to unite mankind with God once more. This is the event which the
Catholic Mass makes present, whatever the rite,
throughout the world and throughout the centuries. A.
Baumstark, perhaps the greatest liturgical scholar of
this century, expressed this well when he wrote that
every worshipper taking part in this liturgy: " feels
himself to be at the point which links those who before
him, since the very earliest days of Christianity, have
offered prayer and sacrifice with those who in time to
come will be offering the same prayer and the same
sacrifice, long after the last fragment of his mortal
remains have crumbled into dust."[25]

Those who reflect upon the nature of the mystery of
the Mass will wonder how men dare to celebrate it,
how a priest dares to utter the words of consecration
which makes the sacrifice of Calvary present, how even
the most saintly layman dares to set foot in the building
where it is being offered—*Terribilis est locus iste : hic
domus Dei est, et porta coeli : et vocabitur aula Dei.*

("Awesome is this place: it is the house of God, and the gate of heaven ; and it shall be called the court of God.")[26] It is natural that the Church, the steward of these holy mysteries, should clothe them with the most solemn and beautiful rites and ceremonies possible. It is equally natural that the book containing these rites should appropriate to itself some of the wonder and veneration evoked by the mysteries themselves. There can be do doubt that the leaders of the authentic liturgical movement in this century regarded the Missal of St. Pius V with much veneration. This veneration for the Missal is well expressed by Dom Cabrol:

". . . the Missal being concerned directly with the Mass and the Holy Eucharist, which is the chief of the Sacraments, has the most right to our veneration, and with it the Pontifical and the Ritual, because those three in the early Church formed one volume as we have seen when speaking of the Sacramentary.

" The Church herself seems to teach us by her actions the reverence in which the Missal should be held. At High Mass it is carried by the deacon in solemn procession to read from it the Gospel of the day. He incenses it as a sign of respect, and it is kissed by a priest as containing the very word of God Himself.

" In the Middle Ages every kind of art was lavished upon it. It was adorned with delicate miniatures, with the most beautifully executed writing and lettering, and bound between sheets of ivory, or even silver and gold, and was studded with jewels like a precious reliquary.

" The Missal has come into being gradually through the course of centuries always carefully guarded by the Church lest any error should slip into it. It is a summary of the authentic teaching of the Church, it reveals the true significance of the mystery which is accomplished in the Mass, and of the prayers which the Church uses."

Dom Cabrol also pays tribute to the incomparable beauty of the Missal from the literary and aesthetic point of view. He stresses that this is not a question of art for art's sake but " we know that truth cannot exist without beauty . . . The beauty of prayer consists in the true and sincere expression of deep sentiment. The Church has never disdained this beauty of form which follows as a consequence of truth ; the great Cathedrals on which in past ages she lavished all the marvels of art stand witness to this . . ."

The historical value of the Missal as a living link with the earliest and formative roots of Christian civilization in Europe is another point to which Dom Cabrol draws attention.

" If these evidences of antiquity were merely a question of archaeology we could not enlarge upon them here, but they have another immense importance. They prove the perpetuity of the Church and the continuity of her teaching. We have life by our tradition, but the Western Church has never confused fidelity to tradition with antiquarianism ; she lives and grows with the times, ever advancing towards her goal ; the liturgy of the Missal with its changes and developments throughout the centuries is a proof of this, but it proves also that the Church does not deny her past ; she possesses a treasure from which she can draw the new and the old and this is the secret of her adaptability which is recognized even by her enemies.

" Though she adopts certain reforms she never forgets her past history and guards preciously her relics of antiquity.

" Here we have the explanation of the growing respect for the liturgy and of the great liturgical revival which we see in these days. *What we may call the ' archaisms' of the Missal are the expression of the faith of our fathers which it is our duty to watch over and hand on to posterity."*

This was the authentic spirit of the Catholic liturgical movement, wholly in accord with the principles described in Chapter IX and in total contrast to the spirit manifested by the Protestant Reformers. It was above all the theological content of the Missal which won the praise of Dom Cabrol—for precisely the opposite reasons which made it unacceptable to the Reformers.

" A Pope in the fifth century, in the course of a

famous controversy, pronounced the following words
which have been regarded, ever since, as an axiom of
theology: *Legem credendi lex statuat supplicandi* (let
the law of prayer fix the law of faith)—in other words,
the liturgy of the Church is a sure guide to her teaching.
Above all else the Church prizes the integrity of the
faith of which she is the guardian: she could not therefore allow her official prayer and worship to be in
contradiction with her doctrine. Thus, she has ever
watched over the formulae of her liturgy with the
utmost care, correcting or rejecting anything that seemed
to be in any way tainted with error. The liturgical
books are, therefore, an authentic expression of the
Catholic faith, and are, in fact, a source from which
theologians may in all security, draw their arguments
in defense of the faith. The liturgy holds an important
place among the *loci theologici,* and in this respect its
principal representative is the Missal. The latter is
not, of course, a manual of Dogmatic Theology, and it
is concerned with the worship of God and not with the
controversial questions. It is nonetheless true that in
the Missal we have a magnificent synthesis of Christian
doctrine—the Holy Eucharist, Sacrifice, prayer, Christian
worship, the Incarnation, and Redemption, in fact, in it
all dogmas of the Faith find expression."

It should not be a matter of surprise that when St.
Pius V finally codified the rites of the Roman Mass he
enshrined the jewel of our faith in a setting of more
than human perfection, a mystic veil worthy of the
divine mystery it enveloped. It would have been surprising had this not been the case with the liturgy
surrounding the sacred act that lies at the heart of the
religion founded by God the Son to the glory of God
the Father and guided and inspired by God the Holy
Ghost. "That overruling influence of the Spirit of
God, that directs even in secondary matters the affairs
of the Church, nowhere else appears so marked and
evident as in the arrangement of the rite of the Holy
Mass, which . . . in its present state forms such a beautiful, perfect whole, yes, a splendid work that excites the
admiration of every reflecting mind. Even the bitterest

adversaries of the Church do not deny it ; unprejudiced aesthetic judges of good taste admit that even from their own standpoint the Mass is to be classed as one of the greatest masterpieces ever composed."[27]

In his book, *This is the Mass,* H. Daniel-Rops explains that it was " declared in the Catechism of the Council of Trent that no part of the Missal ought to be considered *vain* or *superfluous* ; that not even the least of its phrases is to be thought wanting or insignificant. The shortest of its formularies, phrases which take no more than a few seconds to pronounce, form integral parts of a whole wherein are drawn together and set forth God's gift, Christ's sacrifice, and the grace which is showered upon us. This whole conception has in view a sort of spiritual symphony in which themes are taken as being expressed, developed, and unified under the guidance of one purpose."[28]

The beauty, the worth, the perfection of the Roman liturgy of the Mass, so universally acknowledged and admired, was described by Fr. Faber as " the most beautiful thing this side of heaven. It came forth out of the grand mind of the Church, and lifted us out of self, and wrapped us round in a cloud of mystical sweetness and the sublimities of a more than angelic liturgy, and purified us almost without ourselves, and charmed us with celestial charming, so that our very senses seem to find vision, hearing fragrance, taste and touch beyond what earth can give."[29]

This divinely inspired masterpiece was, with a few unimportant variations, the liturgy that formed the object of the hatred and fury of the revolution described in Chapter VIII. The details of its destruction are set out in Chapters XI to XIII. When Laszlo Toth attacked the Pieta of Michelangelo in 1972, the world was horrified. Believer and unbeliever alike were united in their sense of outrage. " How could anyone raise a hand against anything so beautiful?" was the question everyone asked. How men who were priests and even bishops could raise their hands to destroy " the most beautiful thing this side of heaven " is a question that cannot be answered in human terms. Although it was the Sarum and not the Roman rite Mass which Cranmer destroyed, sufficient has already been written in this chapter to demonstrate that not only were they identical in essence but in innumerable particulars.

The Introit for the Feast of the English and Welsh Martyrs begins with a verse from Psalm 28:

" O God, the heathens are come into Thy inheritance : they have defiled Thy holy temple ; they have made Jerusalem as a place to keep fruit."

There is really little to add to this except to note that, by what may not be a coincidence, this feast on 4th May is followed on 5th May by that of Pope St. Pius V in which the Collect thanks God " Who for the overthrowing of the enemies of Thy Church and for the restoring of the beauty of Thy worship, didst choose blessed Pius as supreme Pontiff."

Chapter XI

PREPARATORY MEASURES

MGR. HUGHES has provided an excellent picture of the religious life of the British people on the eve of the Reformation, and what he writes with regard to the Mass is applicable until the accession of the young King Edward VI in 1547. Henry VIII had shown himself very conservative as regards changing the established forms of worship.

Each Sunday, Mgr. Hughes explains, all went to their parish church for Mass, "a sacrifice really offered by the priest, offered in the name of the Church, and also offered by him as the human agent of the great real offerer, the Divine priest, Jesus Christ Himself ; a sacrifice in which the victim was Jesus Christ. The Mass was Christ once again offering Himself to the Father as a propitiation for the sins of the world, not in order to *merit* forgiveness for them, as at Calvary, on the Cross, but in order to provide particular men with a means of making that forgiveness their own, in order that the merit won by the Cross should be applied. Sunday, from the earliest times, had been with Catholics what the Sabbath was—is—to the Jews ; the day of the Lord, consecrated by the testimony of the whole community present at a ritual worship, and by their abstinence from ordinary toil. The neglect to assist at Mass on Sundays and on these special feast days was held a serious sin, as also was the neglect to observe the law forbidding ordinary work on these days.

" Around the church there were placed statues of the saints and painted on the walls, pictures that told the story of the great events narrated in the Scriptures or in the lives of saints. One very favourite subject was the Last Judgement, Christ at the last day of all, judging mankind. Very notable among the saints were the special patron of the particular church or village, the saints traditionally associated with that countryside, above all others, a saint in a class apart, Mary, the Mother of the God-Man, Jesus Christ.

" These churches, generally, were the great pride of the village, for their statues and pictures and silken hangings, for some speciality in a vestment, or in the chalice and other sacred vessels."[1]

A number of means were employed to prepare the people for the replacement of this traditional Latin Mass by a vernacular Protestant Communion service.

THE PRESS

In order to overthrow the Mass, and with it all that remained of the Catholic Faith, the Reformers adopted a cautious approach. They realised that an open frontal attack could rebound on themselves. The way was first prepared with the help of the Press. In 1547 a campaign against the Mass was initiated alleging among other things that " such as honour the bread there for God do no less idolatory than they that made the sun their god or stars."

Gardiner complained that " certain printers, players, and preachers make a wonderment, as though we knew not yet how to be justified, nor what sacraments we should have."[2] The authorities expressed disapproval in public but their failure to take any active steps to suppress these books made it obvious where their sympathies lay. By the end of the year the floodgates were opened and books began to appear filled with abuse of everything Catholic—and even dedicated to the king himself and the Lord Protector. The Blessed Sacrament is described as " a vile cake to be made God and Man " and the Mass as " the worshipping of God made of fine flour." Many of these books were written by continental reformers, among them Luther, Zwingli,

Calvin, Melancthon, Bullinger, Urbanus Regius, Osiander, Hegendorp and Bodius.[3] While these books shocked and outraged most of the ordinary faithful and parish clergy, they made a great impression on those who liked to consider themselves an educated and enlightened élite—almost invariably men of influence in some sphere or other.

Those wishing to defend the Mass found it very difficult to do so as the Reformers had total control of the means of communication. " Here and there possibly a book might be published bearing the name of an author and printer which was distasteful to Cranmer and the Council, but there can be no doubt that this would be done at the peril of those concerned. And as a fact on examining the bibliography of these years it is remarkable that hardly a single book or pamphlet written in support of the ancient doctrines appears to have been issued from the English press. Such treatises as those of Gardiner and Tunstall on the Sacrament had to be printed abroad and in secret.

" On the other hand, the country was flooded with works, either translations of the labours of foreign reformers, or original compositions, inveighing against Catholic observances and specially against the Mass. These bore the name of author or printer and were mostly of the booklet class, which could be sold for a few pence and were evidently designed for wide circulation among the people. In the circumstances there can be no doubt whatever that this style of literature, which is so abundant, could not have had currency without the connivance or good will of the government, and that it really represented beyond question their wishes and intentions. Nor merely was the circulation of such literature, which is chiefly of a profane and scurrilous character, not prohibited or even moderated by any of the numerous proclamations of the time, but express licence was given to printers of such works."[4]

THE PULPIT

Another effective means of propagating the revolutionary ideas was through sermons—preachers with a licence from Cranmer could go from town to town attacking beliefs which, in theory, he still held himself and was upholding. Under Henry for example, while "men and women were dying for beliefs which the Archbishop privately shared, he subscribed to the ruling orthodoxy and imposed it upon others."[5]   While the Reformer-dominated King's Council issued proclamations forbidding irreverent attacks upon the Sacrament, and listing punishments for those who did so, in practice it could be called a "round robin" or "Jack in the box" with impunity. One preacher with Cranmer's licence —Thomas Hancock—was arrested after saying, among other things, "that which the priest holdeth over his head you do see and you kneel before it, you honour it and make an idol of it and you yourselves are most horrible idolators." He was completely discharged at the instigation of the Protector Somerset himself. Cranmer alone had the power of granting a licence to preach and his attitude can best be seen by quoting from an instruction issued by the Privy Council to licensed preachers in June, 1548, forbidding them to bring "that into contempt and hatred which the prince doth either allow or is content to suffer," but at the same time permitting "the lively teaching of the word of God by sermons made after such sort as for the time the Holy Ghost shall put into the preacher's mind."[6]

In his famous sermon "of the plough" preached at St. Paul's on 18th January, 1548, Latimer openly attacked Catholic practices before the whole court, declaring them and the Mass itself to be the work of the devil whose "office is to hinder religion, to maintain superstitution, to set up idolatory, to teach all kinds of popery . . . where the devil is resident, and hath his plough going, there away with books, and up with candles ; away with bibles, and up with beads, away with the light of the Gospel, and up with the light of candles yea at noon-day . . . Where the devil is resident, that he may prevail, up with all superstition and idolatory; censing, painting of images, candles, palms, ashes, holy water and new services of men's inventing . . . Let all things be done in Latin: there must be nothing but Latin . . ."[7]

LITURGICAL INNOVATIONS

This policy of upholding the traditional faith in theory while allowing it to be undermined in practice extended to liturgical innovations. ". . . on the one hand the Council were issuing orders to restrain innovations in the liturgy and on the other were allowing it to be understood that such innovations were not displeasing to them . . ."[8] Cranmer's programme for overthrowing the established liturgy described at the beginning of this chapter was divided into four stages. It has already been explained in Chapter VIII why he deemed it imprudent to do too much too soon. *Stage one* was to have certain portions of the unchanged traditional Mass in the vernacular. *Stage two* was to introduce new material into the old Mass, none of which would be specifically heretical. *Stage three* was to replace the old Mass with an English Communion service which, once more, was not specifically heretical. *Stage four* was to replace this service with a specifically Protestant one. As will be explained in Chapter XVI, the psychology of this process was very sound. Very few men have the courage to be martyrs and even those with strong convictions are liable to seek a compromise where one is possible. Such a compromise was possible with each of Cranmer's first three stages—and once the process of compromising has been entered into it tends to be self-perpetuating. A man who has been making continual concessions is liable to lack the will to make a stand and to feel that, " in any case it is too late now ". Prominent among the liturgical innovations which prepared the way for or accompanied the 1549 Prayer Book were the principles that the liturgy must be in the vernacular and audible throughout; Communion under both kinds; a new order of Communion to be used with the old Mass; the replacement of altars with tables.

THE VERNACULAR AND AUDIBILITY

Although a number of the Reformers began by using a modified traditional or newly composed Latin liturgy it soon became a *sine qua non* of Protestantism (but for some Lutherans) that worship must be exclusively in the vernacular.[9]   Statements such as the following, taken from the writings of the Reformers and *condemned* by Trent, provide an accurate summary of the Protestant standpoint: "The rite of the Church of Rome by which the words of consecration are said secretly and in a low voice is to be condemned and the Mass ought to be celebrated only in the vernacular language which all understand."[10]   The use of the vernacular even before the introduction of the new services was, in itself, "indeed a revolution".[11]   It was also an effective instrument for revolutionary change as it accustomed the people to the idea of drastic change in their manner of worship.   Where the ordinary Catholic was concerned, Cranmer's revision of the Latin Mass in his *new rite* of 1549 did not appear as startling as the transition from Latin to English while still using the old rite.   Even an Anglican author can see clearly that by introducing English into the traditional services "Cranmer clearly was preparing for the day when liturgical revision would become possible".[12]

As early as 11th April, 1547, Compline was being sung in English in the royal chapel.[13]   The opening of the first Parliament of Edward's reign was made the occasion for a far more significant novelty as it touched the ritual of the Mass itself.   The King rode from his palace of Westminster to the church of St. Peter with all the lords spiritual and temporal for a Mass during which the *Gloria, Credo* and *Agnus Dei* were all sung in English.[14]   Even the more conservative bishops were now prepared to concede that while Latin should still be the general rule during Mass, especially " in the mysteries thereof, nevertheless certain prayers might be in the mother tongue for the instruction and stirring of the devotion of the people as shall be thought convenient."[15] By 12th May, 1548, it was possible to have a totally English Mass at Westminster, including the consecration.[16]

" It is difficult," writes A. L. Rowse, " for anyone without a knowledge of anthropology to appreciate fully the astonishing audacity, the profound disturbance to the unconscious levels upon which society lives its life, of such an action as the substitution of an English liturgy for the age-long Latin rite of Western Christendom in which Englishmen had been swaddled time out of mind . . . nothing can detract from the revolutionary audacity of such an interference with the customary, the subconscious, the ritual element in life."[17]

As well as insisting upon the vernacular, the Reformers demanded that the whole service should be audible to the congregation. A rubric in the 1549 Prayer Book requires that the priest " shall saye, or syng, playnly and distinctly, this prayer folowyng ", namely, the Canon.[18]

The Council of Trent pronounced anathemas upon anyone holding the propositions either that " the rite of the Roman Church whereby a part of the Canon and the words of consecration are pronounced in a low tone is to be condemned ; or that the Mass ought to be celebrated in the vernacular tongue only."[19] These anathemas do not, of course, preclude the possibility of these practices being permitted within the Roman rite.

COMMUNION UNDER BOTH KINDS

One of Cranmer's first important innovations was to impose the practice of Communion under both kinds for the laity at the end of 1547. Many Catholics both in England and abroad made the mistake of conceding this change without opposition for the sake of peace. " It was after all only a matter of ecclesiastical discipline, although some innovators in urging the incompleteness of the Sacrament, when administered under one kind only, gave a doctrinal turn to the question which issued in heresy. The great advantages secured to the innovators by the adoption of communion under both kinds in England was the opportunity it afforded them of effecting a break with the ancient missal."[20] Every such break with tradition lessened the impact of those to follow so that when changes that were not simply matters of discipline were introduced the possibility of effective resistance was considerably lessened.

THE NEW ORDER OF COMMUNION

The printing of "The Order of Communion"—a booklet of only three or four leaves—was finished on 8th March, 1548. This was to be used in conjunction with the traditional Mass and must not be confused with the wholly new Communion service contained in the 1549 Prayer Book. The 1548 rite contained exhortations addressed to those about to receive the Sacrament which, according to Mgr. Hughes, contained " ambiguities designed to make the rite one which could be conscientiously used by those who did not believe that He (Christ) was there present except to the communicant in the moment of receiving Holy Communion, and who believed that the presence, even at that moment, was not in what was received but only in ' the heart' of the receiver."[21] The book also included a ritual for the administration of Communion under both kinds and these prayers, with a few modifications, were incorporated into the 1549 Book of Common Prayer. Mgr. Hughes' assessment of the ambiguous nature of the new rite is shared by the Protestant historian S. T. Bindoff. " The new service contained little or nothing clearly inconsistent with Catholic doctrine. At the crucial points its phraseology was ambiguous, and the statute embodying it explicitly renounced any intention of condemning rites used elsewhere."[22]

Just how pleasing this new rite was to discerning Protestants was made clear by no less a person than Miles Coverdale who translated it into Latin and sent a copy to Calvin declaring it to be " the first fruits of godliness (according as the Lord now wills his religion to revive in England) . . ."[23]

In his proclamation giving effect to the new service the King admonishes such radical Protestants as Coverdale " to stay and quiet themselves with this our direction—and not enterprise to run afore and so by their rashness to become the greatest hinderers" of change. But at the same time he speaks of a " most earnest intent further to travail for the reformation and setting forth of such godly orders."[24]

The radicals did not need to " quiet themselves" long and the further " godly orders" were to be imposed in the following year.

ALTARS REPLACED BY TABLES

This was another step directly in line with the liturgical policies of the continental Reformers, the final product of which is well summarized by a description of the Communion service at Strassburg after 1530 when Bucer's influence became dominant. " So, mass, priest, and altar are replaced by Lord's Supper, minister and Holy Table, and the westward replaces the eastward position of the celebrant."[25] (It is worth repeating that Bucer influenced Cranmer, and hence his new liturgy, more than any other continental reformer.) On the same theme, Calvin explains that God " has given us a table at which to feast, not an altar on which to offer sacrifice, He has not consecrated priests, but ministers to distribute the sacred banquet."[26]

The wholesale destruction of altars in England did not take place until after the imposition of the 1549 Prayer Book, but a start had been made in 1548 with the altars of the chantry chapels which Cranmer had suppressed. After 1549 the stone altars upon which the Sacrifice of the Mass had been offered were replaced with wooden tables placed in the chancel. On 27th November, 1548, John ab Ulmis wrote to Bullinger as follows: " At this time those privileged altars are entirely overthrown in a great part of England, and by the common consent of the higher classes altogether abolished. Why should I say more? Those idolatrous altars are now become hogsties (Arae factae sunt harae), that is the habitation of swine and beasts."[27]

During a vacancy in the See of Norwich when it came under Cranmer's jurisdiction (1549-1550), " The most part of all altars " in this diocese were taken down.[28] In a series of Lenten sermons preached before the King and Council Hooper urged the complete abolition of altars and the substitution of tables because there were only three forms of sacrifice which Christian men could offer and these did not require an altar. They were sacrifices of thanksgiving ; benevolence and liberality to the poor ; and the mortifying of our own bodies, and to die unto sin . . . " If we study not daily to offer these sacrifices to God, we be no Christian men. *Seeing Christian men have none other sacrifice than these, which may and ought to be done without altars, there should among Christians be no altars."* While altars remained, he insisted, " both the ignorant people, and the ignorant and evil-persuaded priest, will dream always of sacrifice."[29]

On 27th March, 1550, after the appointment of Ridley to the See of London, Hooper wrote to Bullinger: " He will, I hope, destroy the altars of Baal, as he did heretofore in his church when he was Bishop of Rochester. I can scarcely express to you, my very dear friend, under what difficulties and dangers we are labouring and struggling, that the idol of the Mass may be thrown out." He was able to add, " Many altars have been destroyed in this city (London) since I arrived here."[30] Hooper's expectations of Ridley proved to be well founded. Within three months he had issued injunctions calling for the removal of the altars from the churches of his diocese.[31] Altars were " too enduring monuments " to " the age old belief in the sacrifice of the Mass. Altar-smashing was already a well recog-

nised mark of the Reformation on the Continent, where
the practice had been the normal accompaniment of the
abolition of the Mass."[32]   On 24th November, 1550, the
King's Council ordered the universal implementation of
this policy in England, "that all the altars throughout
the kingdom should be destroyed.   For the future,
whenever the rite of the Holy Eucharist was celebrated, a
wooden table was to be used, covered, during the rite,
with a cloth of linen.[33]   This was intended "to avoid
all matters of further contention and strife", and in a
set of reasons accompanying the instruction (signed by
Cranmer among others) it was explained that: "First,
the form of a table shall more move the simple from
the superstitious opinions of the Popish Mass unto the
right use of the Lord's Supper.   For the use of an
altar is to make sacrifice upon it: the use of a table
is to serve for men to eat upon.   Now when we come
again unto the Lord's board, what do we come for?
To sacrifice Christ again, and to crucify him again ; or
to feed upon him that was once only crucified and
offered up for us?   If we come to feed upon him,
spiritually to eat his body, and spiritually to drink his
blood, which is the true use of the Lord's Supper ; then
no man can deny but the form of a table is more meet
for the Lord's board than the form of an altar."[34]

   "Then throughout the land the consecrated altars of
the Christian sacrifice were cast out, and in the account
books of country parishes such items as this appeared:
'Payd to tylers for breckynge downe forten awters in
the cherche' . . ."[35]

   A descendant of Bishop Ridley writes in a biography
of his reforming ancestor that the destruction of the
altars which the ordinary people considered sacrilege
shocked them into a full realization of the extent of the
revolution which had taken place: ". . . the removal
of altars brought home to every subject in the kingdom
that the central object which had stood in the churches
for over a thousand years, and which they had watched
with awe every Sunday since their early childhood, was
condemned as idolatrous and thrown contemptuously
away by the adherents of the new religion which had

been forced upon them."[36]

The fact that the word altar is used in certain of the
rubrics of the 1549 Prayer Book might appear to involve
some inconsistency with the teaching of the Reformers.
This point is dealt with in the explanation which accompanied the order of the King's Council demanding the
destruction of altars. It explains that "it calleth the
table where the holy Communion is distributed, with
lauds and thanksgiving unto the Lord, an altar ; for
that there is offered the same sacrifice of praise and
thanksgiving."[37]   Nevertheless, the word 'altar' was
struck out of the 1552 Prayer Book and was not subse-
quently replaced.   Archbishop Laud ordered the
communion tables to be placed altar-wise, against the
east wall, in about 1636.[38]

There were a good number of other innovations some
of which might appear of minor importance but nonetheless played their part in contributing to the general
atmosphere of change, disturbance, and unrest.   The
most important of these was the widespread destruction of statues.   The Reformers abolished such well
loved ceremonies as the carrying of candles on Candle-
mas day, the distribution of ashes on Ash Wednesday
and of palms on Palm Sunday.[39] "In these years 1547
and 1548 consequently the popular mind was being
stirred up by changes in old established ceremonial, by
novel introductions into the services, by intemperate
preaching and by profane tracts scattered broadcast
over the country, attacking with scurrilous abuse what
the people had hitherto been taught to regard as the
Most Holy."[40]

The seeds of revolution had been sown. All that
remained was for the revolutionaries to reap their
harvest.

Chapter XII

AN INGENIOUS ESSAY IN AMBIGUITY

IN THEIR vindication of the Bull *Apostolicae Curae,* the English Catholic bishops urged a comparison of the Missal with Cranmer's 1549 Prayer Book which would reveal a series of omissions " of which the evident purpose was to eliminate the idea of sacrifice."[1] As has been shown in previous chapters, although this prayer book replaced the Sarum Missal the nature of these omissions can be made clear by comparing it with the Roman Missal in view of the substantial identity between the Sarum and Roman rites. The texts of the 1549 Prayer Book and the Sarum Missal are both obtainable.[2]

Cranmer entitled his new service " The Supper of the Lorde and the Holy Communion, commonly called the Masse." This title is an adequate summary of its nature —it could be, and was clearly intended to be, interpreted as a Protestant " commemoration " of the Lord's Supper but contained nothing specifically heretical and could be interpreted as a Mass. The word " Mass " was, of course, dropped from the title of the service in the 1552 Prayer Book which marked the fourth and final stage in Cranmer's liturgical revolution, the imposition of a service which could be interpreted as nothing but a Protestant commemoration. This ambiguity is stressed by Francis Clark in the most authoritative study of the Eucharistic doctrine of the Reformers yet undertaken, in which he quotes the Protestant scholar T. M. Parker:

" The first Prayer Book of Edward VI could not be convicted of overt heresy, for it was adroitly framed and contained no express denial of pre-Reformation doctrine. It was, as an Anglican scholar puts it, ' an ingenious essay in ambiguity ', purposely worded in such a manner that the more conservative could place their own construction upon it and reconcile their consciences to using it, while the Reformers would interpret it in their own sense and would recognise it as *an instrument for furthering* the next stage of the religious revolution."[3]

Professor A. G. Dickens assesses Cranmer's service as follows: "Though wholly in the English language, this Prayer Book remained a masterpiece of compromise, even of studied ambiguity. While it did not specifically deny Catholic doctrine, its ambiguous phrases were understood by its author in a Protestant sense and was intended to enable Protestants to use it with good conscience."[4]   Another Protestant historian, S. T. Bindoff comments: "Its keynote was compromise, and in that it faithfully reflected the personality of its chief author.   It also reflected his mastery of the language. Melancthon had once told Cranmer that ' in church it is more proper to call a spade a spade than to throw ambiguous expressions before posterity '."[5]

Ample documentation has been provided in Chapter VIII to demonstrate that the " reformed " liturgies in general, and the 1549 Prayer Book in particular, expressed their Protestant ethos principally by what they rejected from the traditional Latin Mass—everything that smacked of oblation, as Luther expressed it.[6]

" The liturgy of the 1549 Book of Common Prayer has been exhaustively studied, and there is wide agreement that its most significant difference in comparison with the Latin rite which it replaced was the omission of sacrificial language."[7]   This can be made clear by examining Cranmer's Communion service in some detail.

The Supper of the Lorde and the Holy Communion, Commonly called the Masse
1549

" Even the closest theological scrutiny of the new composition will not detect anything inconsistent with, or excluding, Luther's negation of the sacrificial nature of the Mass.

"Looking therefore at the characteristics of the new Anglican service and contrasting it on the one hand with the ancient missal, and on the other with the Lutheran liturgies, there can be no hesitation whatever in classing it with the latter, not with the former," writes Cardinal Gasquet.[8] For this reason, it will be pertinent to refer to Luther's liturgical innovations while examining Cranmer's service.

(a) The first part of his new rite corresponds very closely with Luther's 1523 Latin Mass. Luther stipulated that vestments still in use could continue to be used, also the word Mass. The service was to begin with the Introit (the whole psalm to be sung), the *Judica me,* with its reference to the priest going "to the altar of God", and the *Confiteor* are both abolished.[9] The confession of sins to Our Lady, the saints and angels and the request for their intercession was obviously incompatible with the Protestant doctrine of Justification. It was also regarded, from the Lutheran standpoint, as a sacerdotal preparation for the sacrifice.[10] Cranmer follows Luther in omitting it.

(b) "Next, according to Luther, there are to follow the *Kyrie, Gloria,* and the ancient collects (provided they are pious), the Epistle, Gradual, Gospel and Nicene Creed." Cranmer follows this pattern but abolishes the Gradual.

(c) Luther says that a sermon may be preached before the Mass or after the *Credo.* Cranmer follows the latter suggestion and adds two exhortations to Holy Communion taken from the 1548 Order of Communion referred to in Chapter XI. Certain modifications had been made in these exhortations to make their Protestant import more clear.

(d) After this there follows in the "Roman Mass" what Luther describes as "all that abomination called the Offertory, and from this point almost everything stinks of oblation". Luther therefore swept away the

whole of the Offertory in the Roman rite and Cranmer
followed suit. " The ' Offertory ' now became merely
the collecting of money for ' the poor men's box ' and
for church dues. Gone were all the prayers and invoca-
tions of the former Latin rite which spoke of the sacrifice to be performed."[11]   A Communion Antiphon is still
said or sung " according to the length and shortness of
the tyme, that the people be offering."   There is no
trace of such prayers as the following from the Sarum
Missal: " Receive, O Holy Father, this Oblation which
I, an unworthy sinner offer in Thine honour, of Blessed
Mary and all Thy saints, for my sins and offences, and
for the salvation of the living and of all the Faithful
departed."

(e) *The Orate Fratres* and the Secret Prayer are
abolished both by Luther and Cranmer.   Both direct
that after completing the preparation of the bread and
wine the minister should begin the *Sursum Corda*
dialogue preceding the Preface.   Dialogue and Preface
are as in the Roman rite and in Cranmer's rite this
similarity is enhanced by keeping the *Sanctus* in its
traditional position.   Luther had postponed it until after
the Words of Institution, though this was not always
observed.

(f) The most startling difference between the 1549
Prayer Book and Luther's 1523 Mass is that the former
keeps a version of the Canon while Luther had cast
aside " everything that savours of oblation together with
the entire Canon, let us keep those things which are pure
and holy."   However, from what Cranmer kept of the
Old Mass " all the numerous references indicating and
implying that the action being done is a sacrifice, and
that what the priest is offering as a sacrifice, is the
Body and Blood of Christ here really present—all this
has been carefully cut out ".   Cardinal Gasquet explains
that: " Luther swept away the Canon altogether and
retained only the essential words of Institution.
Cranmer substituted a new prayer of about the same
length as the old Canon, leaving in it a few shreds of

the ancient one, but divesting it of its character of sacrifice and oblation."[12]   Some examples of Cranmer's technique are provided here:

(i) The opening prayer of the Roman Canon—the *Te Igitur*—asks God " to receive and bless these gifts, these offerings, these holy and unblemished sacrifices." Cranmer asks God " to receive these our praiers, which we offer unto thy diuine Majestie."

(ii) The prayer *Hanc Igitur* before the Consecration asks God to accept " The oblation which we, Thy servants and Thy whole family make to Thee . . ." Cranmer replaces this by a reference to the " full, perfect, and sufficient sacrifyce, oblacion, and satysfacyon for the sinnes of the whole world which Christ made upon the Cross."

(iii) Before the words of Consecration Cranmer asks God to " blesse and sanctifie these thy gyftes, and creatures of bread and wyne, that they maie *be unto us* the bodye and bloode of thy moste derely beloued sonne Jesus Christ."   Hugh Ross Williamson has pointed out that though a similar phrase occurs in the traditional prayer immediately preceding the Consecration (*Quam oblationem*), " the transubstantiation has been prepared for by the magnificent *Te Igitur, Memento Domine* and *Hanc Igitur* where the ' holy, unblemished sacrificial gifts ' are described in terms proper to the coming change into the Body and Blood of which we are the unworthy beneficiaries."[13]   Fr. Messenger stresses the fact that Cranmer's rite says " may *be* unto us " while the Roman rite has " fiant ", namely, that they may *become* or *be made* for us.   The former is clearly intended to exclude the idea of change but even " fiant " could quite easily have been interpreted in a Protestant sense if not prepared for by the magnificent prayers to which Mr. Ross Williamson refers.   They would *be* Christ's Body and Blood in a Protestant sense, having *become* so by the faith of the communicant who would be spiritually nourished by receiving them as food and drink. In reply to Gardiner who insisted upon interpreting the 1549 rite in the orthodox sense, Cranmer explained ". . . we do not pray absolutely that the bread and wine may be made the body and blood of Christ, but that unto us in the holy mystery they may be so, that is to say, that we may worthily receive the same that we may be made partakers of Christ's body and blood, and that therewith in spirit and in truth we may be spiritually nourished."[14]

(iv) Despite the fact that the words of Consecration had been codified by the Council of Florence, Cranmer did not hesitate to make changes even here.[15] A detailed comparison of the two forms is available in Appendix III: Changes in the Words of Consecration. The principal changes made by Cranmer are the addition of the words " which is given for you (*quod pro vobis tradetur*), do this in remembrance of Me " after the Consecration of the bread ; the removal of the words *Mysterium Fidei* from the consecration of the wine, and the translation of *benedixit* as " blessed and given thanks." This word was considered of great significance by the Reformers as they considered that a literal translation of *benedicere* as " to bless " clearly implied Transubstantiation. As Ridley explains: " Innocentius, a bishop of Rome of the latter days and Duns Scotus do attribute this work (i.e. Transubstantiation) unto the word *benedixit* ' He blessed '."[16] The conservative English bishops also laid stress on the translation of *benedicere* as " to bless ". " Worcester said once to me," writes Latimer, " that to offer was contained in *benedicere,* which is not true, for *benedicere* is to give thanks."[17] This is not the place for a discussion of the precise theological significance of the word *benedixit* in the Consecration formula. For the purpose of this study it is sufficient to note the significance the Reformers attached to it, and the action they took. In the 1549 Prayer Book it was translated as " blessed and given thanks " and in the 1552 Prayer Book the words " blessed and " are left out altogether and have not been restored.

(v) The prayer *Unde et memores* which follows the Consecration in the Roman rite is rewritten in Cranmer's service to exclude mention of the *hostiam puram, hostiam sanctam, hostiam immaculatam*. Similarly, the linking of the Mass with the most celebrated sacrifice of the Old Testament in the prayer *Supra quae* is also removed.

(vi) Cranmer's Canon does contain a commemoration for the dead, very similar in terms to that of the Roman which, in this instance, is not worded in terms specific enough to conflict with the Protestant doctrine that *sola fides justificat*. There is also a commemoration of " the glorious and moste blessed virgin Mary, mother of Thy sonne Jesu Christe our Lord and God, and in the holy Patriarches, Prophets, Apostles and Martyrs . . ." Fr. Messenger is extremely critical of the term " Virgin Mary " in reference to Our Lady as opposed to the " ever-Virgin " of the Roman Canon. The fact that a reference to the perpetual integrity of Our Lady had been *removed* at a time when this doctrine was being called into question could be interpreted as implying that doubts on this teaching were lawful.[18]

(vii) One of the most significant innovations in Cranmer's Canon is the introduction of an epiklesis. The epiklesis is, as now understood, an invocation to the Holy Ghost that He may change the bread and wine into the Body and Blood of Christ. It is a characteristic of the Eastern liturgies and there is no prayer that is clearly of this kind in the Roman Mass.[19] There has been considerable discussion among liturgical historians about whether certain prayers in the Roman Mass could have been an *epiklesis* or, if none of them ever were, whether there once was an *epiklesis* which has been removed. The teaching of the Catholic Church is that " the form of this sacrament are the words of the Saviour with which He effected this sacrament, for the priest effects the sacrament speaking in the person of Christ."[20] It is explained that the words of Consecration bring about the transubstantiation of the bread and wine into the true Body and Blood of Christ. The form of Consecration was specified as that laid down in the Roman Canon.[21] In 1822 Pope Pius VII ordered that no one, not even a bishop or patriarch, should in future dare to defend the position that the *epiklesis* was necessary for consecration. Pope Pius X found it necessary to repeat this instruction in 1910.[22] The *epiklesis* is, of course, found in the Catholic Eastern rites and there can be no possible criticism of such a prayer. The dispute has been a doctrinal one as to whether the *epiklesis* is necessary for consecration. The artificial introduction of an *epiklesis* into a liturgy which had not contained one is what is at issue here. The prayer in question is the one which has already been discussed in (iii) above. The full text reads: "Heare us (o merciful father) we besech thee ; and with thy holy spirite and words vouchsafe to blesse and sanctifie these thy gyftes, and creatures of bread and wyne, that they maie be unto us the bodye and bloude of thy moste derely beloued sonne Jesus Christe." Fr. Messenger considers that this prayer was certainly suggested by the invocation of the Holy Ghost found in Greek liturgies.[23] Needless to say, it is clear that Cranmer did not consider that even with his new *epiklesis* there was anything more than a spiritual presence of Christ.

(viii) Another change which shows "how carefully the new rite was constructed in order to remove traces of the sacrificial concept which had permeated the old", is the replacement of the phrase (from the *Supplices te*) referring to those "who are partakers *at the altar* of the precious Body and Blood of Thy Son . . ."[24] Cranmer changes this to: "Whosoeur shall be partakers of thys holy Communion, maye worthily receive the most precious body and bloude of thy sonne Jesus Christ."

(g) Luther kept the *Pater Noster* with the traditional introduction but omitted the *Libera Nos* with its invocation of the intercession of Our Lady and the saints. He also omitted the Fraction of the Host. Cranmer followed suit.

(h) Luther directed that the *Agnus Dei* should be sung during the Communion. Cranmer followed suit.

(i) Luther had kept the first of the preparatory prayers for Communion in the Roman rite, namely, the prayer for peace and unity beginning *Domine Jesu Christe qui dixisti,* as it contains no reference to the Blessed Sacrament.[25]   Luther omits the second Prayer— *Domine Jesu Christi Fili Dei* which does contain such a reference, together with the third prayer which comes into the same category—the *Perceptio Corporis tui.* The first prayer does not occur in the Sarum Missal but almost identical forms of the second and third do and Cranmer omits these.   In place of the prayer for peace and unity in the Roman rite, the Sarum rite has two most beautiful prayers which are excluded by Cranmer for obvious reasons:

" O Lord, Holy Father, Almighty and everlasting God, grant me worthily to receive this most holy Body and Blood of Thy Son Our Lord Jesus Christ, that I may by it be found worthy to obtain remission of all my sins, and to be filled with the Holy Ghost, and to hold Thy peace. For Thou art God, and there is none beside Thee, whose kingdom and glorious dominion abideth for ever. Amen."

In the second prayer the priest speaks of Christ's flesh " which I unworthy hold in my hands."

(j) Cranmer's service does contain a penitential rite before Communion with a severely truncated *Confiteor* in which the references to Our Lady, the saints, and the angels are removed.

(k) The celebrant's Communion prayers are omitted from Cranmer's rite—those from the Sarum rite being even less acceptable than the Roman: " Hail evermore, most holy flesh of Christ, to me above all things the sum of delight. May the Body of Our Lord Jesus

Christ avail to me a sinner as the way of life." However, Cranmer does include a prayer to be said by the priest in his own name and that of the people which contains phrases more than capable of being interpreted in a Catholic sense.

"Graunt us therefore (gracious lorde so to eate the fleshe of thy dere sonne Jesus Christ, and to drynke his bloud in these holy Misteries, that we may continually dwell in hym, and he in us . . ." It is important to note that the inclusion of such expressions does not necessarily imply an acceptance of the Catholic teaching of the substantial presence of Christ in the Blessed Sacrament, a belief which Cranmer most certainly did not have. Sufficient has already been said on the use of Catholic terms by Protestants in a sense that involves the rejection of the Catholic teaching. (See Chapter VII.) The use of the word " spiritually " is perhaps the best example. Holy Communion can be spoken of as our spiritual food and drink with perfect orthodoxy but it can also be intended to specifically exclude the Catholic teaching of the Real Presence. " For figuratively he is in the bread and wine, and spiritually he is in them that worthily eat and drink the bread and wine ; but really, carnally, and corporally he is only in heaven . . ."[26]

(l) As regards the administration of Holy Communion, it was to be given under both kinds. This had been one of the first changes the Reformers had managed to push through Parliament.[27] The reception of Communion under one kind was, of course, simply a disciplinary matter within the Roman rite. In the Eastern rites Holy Communion is given under both kinds. However, in reverting to a practice which had been long abandoned Cranmer was making the type of revolutionary break with established tradition condemned by the English Bishops in their vindication of *Apostolicae Curae*. (See Chapter VIII.) Cranmer retained the traditional form of altar-bread but one of the rubrics to the 1549 Prayer Book directs that it must be " without all manner of printe, and something more larger and thicker than it was, so that it may be aptly deuided in two pieces, at the leaste, or more, by the discretion of the minister." This would help to stress the new emphasis on the Mass as essentially a commemorative meal.

(m) After the Communion, Luther omits the Ablutions but allows the two prayers *Quod ore sumpsimus* and *Corpus tuum* to be said. Cranmer omits both Ablutions and prayers, the *Corpus tuum* was not included in the Sarum rite but the *Quod ore* was followed by another prayer which he found equally unacceptable.

(n) The most unacceptable prayer after the Communion was quite clearly the *Placeat tibi* " May the homage of my bounden duty be pleasing to Thee, O Holy Trinity ; and grant that the sacrifice which I, though unworthy, have offered in the sight of Thy Majesty may be acceptable to Thee, and through Thy mercy be a propitiation for me and for all those for whom I have offered it."

This prayer had been singled out for particular censure by Protestants and, quite naturally, it vanished both in the Lutheran and Cranmerian rites.[28]

(o) Both Luther and Cranmer end their services with a blessing and omit the Last Gospel.

DISTRIBUTION OF COMMUNION

It is interesting to note that in the 1549 rite the people received Holy Communion while kneeling from the hands of a priest. " And although it bee redde in aunciente writers, that the people many years past receiued at the priestes handes the Sacrament of the body of Christ in thyr owne handes, and no commaundemèt of Christ to the contrary: Yet forasmuche as they many tymes conueyghed the same secretelye away, kept it with them, and diuersly abused it to supersticion and wickednes: lest any suche thynge hereafter should be attempted, and that an uniformitie might be used, throughoute the whole Realme: it is thought conuenient the people commoly receiue the Sacramèt of Christes body, in their mouthes, at the Priestes hande."[29]

However in the 1552 Prayer Book the minister is directed to give the bread " to the people in their handes kneling ".[30] In order that the fact that the communicants were still required to kneel should not be " misconstrued, depraued, and interpreted in a wrong part " the notorious " Black Rubric " was added which explains that: " Leste yet the same kneeling myght be thought or taken otherwyse, we dooe declare that it is not ment thereby, that any adoration is doone, or oughte to be doone, eyther unto the sacramental bread or wyne there bodily receyued, or unto any reall and essencial presence there beeying of Christ's naturall fleshe and bloude. For as concernynge the Sacramentall bread and wyne, they remayne styll in theyr verye naturall substaunces, and therefore may not be adored, for that were Idolatrye to be abhorred by all faythfull christians. And as concernynge the naturall body and blood of our sauiour, Christ, they are in heauen and not here. For it is agaynst the trueth of Christes true naturall bodye, to be in moe places then in one, at one tyme."[31] This rubric was issued as a Royal Proclamation after some copies of the 1552 Prayer Book had already been published. It is interesting to note the correspondence between this rubric and doctrines anathematised in the Canons of the Thirteenth Session of the Council of Trent (1551).

Canon 1. " If anyone denies that the body and blood, together with the soul and divinity, of our Lord Jesus Christ and, therefore, the whole Christ is truly, really, and substantially contained in the Sacrament of the most holy Eucharist, but says that Christ is present in the Sacrament only as in a sign or figure, or by his power: let him be anathema."

Canon 6. " If anyone says that Christ, the only

begotten Son of God is not to be adored in the holy sacrament of the Eucharist with the worship of latria, including the external worship, and that the sacrament, therefore, is not to be honoured with extraordinary festive celebrations nor solemnly carried from place to place in processions according to the praiseworthy universal rite and custom of the holy Church ; or that the Sacrament is not to be publicly exposed for the people's adoration, and that those who adore it are idolators: let him be anathema."[32]

Cranmer was taking careful note of the teaching of Trent and in March, 1552, he wrote to Calvin : " Our adversaries are now holding their councils at Trent for the establishment of their errors . . . They are, as I am informed, making decrees respecting the worship of the host ; therefore we ought to leave no stone unturned, not only that we may guard others against this idolatory, but also that we may ourselves come to an agreement upon the doctrine of this sacrament."[33]

Cranmer's response to the Council of Trent can be found in the Forty-two Articles of 1553 which were basically his work.[34] A passage in Article XXIX is illuminating both with reference to the Black Rubric and to the Canons of Trent's Thirteenth Session which have just been cited. Even E. C. Gibson, an Anglican historian who is prepared to go to any length to inter- pret the Articles in the most Catholic manner possible, is compelled to concede that it reflects the opinion of John a Lasco under whose influence Cranmer had come, " and its teaching on the presence in the Eucharist, if not actually Zwinglianism, is perilously near to it."[35]

The relevant section of Article XXIX reads as follows :

" Transubstanciation, or the chaunge of the sub- stuance of breade and wine into the substaunce of Christes bodie, and bloude cannot be proued by holie writte, but is repugnant to the plaine woordes of Scrip- ture, and hath geuen occasione to many supersticions.

" Forasmoche as the trueth of mannes nature re- quireth, that the bodie of one, and theself same manne cannot be at one time in diuere places, but must nedes be in some one certeine place: Therefore the bodie of Christe cannot bee presente at one time in many, and diuerse places. And because (as holie Scripture doeth teache) Christe was taken vp into heauen, and there shall continue vnto thende of the worlde, a faithful man ought not either to beleue, or openlie to confesse the reall, and bodilie presence (as thei term it) of Christes fleshe and bloude, in the Sacramente of the Lordes Supper.

"The Sacramente of the Lordes Supper was not commanded by Christes ordinaunce to be kepte, carried about, lifted vp, nor worshipped."[36]

E. C. Gibson accepts in his history of the Thirty-Nine Articles that "there can be little doubt that in 1552 and 1553 the formularies of the Church in this country were (to say the least) intended to be acceptable to those who sympathised with the Swiss school of Reformers in regard to the Eucharist, and who held that the Presence was merely figurative."[37]

The "Black Rubric" was omitted in the 1559 Prayer Book but was restored in 1662 with what another Anglican historian, J. T. Tomlinson, describes as a few "merely verbal" alterations. He cites other Anglican historians who also insist that "*no change* of meaning was intended by the verbal alterations of 1662", and points out that: "The pivot sentence upon which the whole Declaration hung remains unchanged, viz. that the body of Christ which '*is*' in heaven, is '*not* HERE.' That was, and is, absolutely fatal to *any* theory of 'presence' in the sense of residence within the elements. It was not merely a corporal *manner* of presence (which no Romanist ever affirmed), but 'ANY corporal presence' at all which is expressly rejected."[38]

It is worth pointing out that the more radical Reformers, such as John Knox and John Hooper, objected to kneeling for Communion no matter what might be said in any rubrics.[39] For them, kneeling could imply adoration, and anything which could even imply adoration should be abolished.

Chapter XIV

" GODLY ORDER " OR " CHRISTMAS GAME " ?

THE REACTION to the new liturgy has already been touched upon in Chapter VIII. It was shown that most of the clergy tended to make use of the ambiguities in the new communion service in an attempt to interpret it in an orthodox manner. This reaction will be examined in detail in the next two chapters. The ordinary faithful did not possess the theological skill to put an orthodox interpretation upon a radical break with the traditions of their forefathers. If the Reformers had no intention of altering the traditional doctrine of the Mass then why had they changed the traditional liturgy? As is so often the case, the intuition of the simple faithful proved to be the most accurate and the most honest. Scholars like Gardiner who tried to show that the new service was compatible with the Catholic doctrine on the Mass could certainly have had no illusions about the beliefs and intentions of Cranmer and his associates. As the Anglican historian J. T. Tomlinson expresses it: ". . . the First Prayer Book was regarded *at that time* as merely provisional until the English Reformers could give full effect to their own predilections."[1]

The changes in religious policy made during the reign of Henry VIII had passed over the heads of the mass of the English people. The suppression of chantries in 1547 and the removal of images had brought the nature of Protestantism home to every parish. The imposition of the new communion service proved to be the last straw in some cases, and it provoked a number of armed risings.

Like all reformers, those who had devised and imposed the new liturgy were confident that they knew what was best for the people. "The services must be understood by the people and made congregational, the people must be turned from spectators intent upon their private devotions into active participants."[2] The new service became mandatory on 9th June, 1549, Whitsunday. However the congregational activity which it evoked was not exactly of the kind which Cranmer had intended. The parishioners of Sampford Courtenay—a beautiful granite church on the edge of Dartmoor—"heard it read and did not like it, and on the following day they compelled their parish priest to return to the old ritual. They likened the new service to 'a Christmas game' and would have no changes until the king was of full age."[3] A contemporary Protestant historian complained that the parish priest "yielded to their wills and forthwith raversheth himself in his old popish attire and sayeth mass and all such services as in times past accustomed."[4]

Local justices of the peace came to remonstrate with the peasants—but it was of no avail. One was so tactless that a farmer named Letherbridge struck him with his billhook and others "fell upon him and slew him . . ."[5] The west country men were in no mood for argument, in fact they were not really competent to argue. They were making a stand for something which deep within them they knew was right ; it involved their roots and their eternal destiny. Scholars could, and would, belittle them. Cranmer could, and would, sneer at them—but it is not always those who are able to put the best reasons for their cause who are in the right.

The news spread "as a cloud carried with a violent wind and as a thunder clap sounding through the whole country and the common people so well allowed and liked thereof that they clapped their hands for joy."[6] The Mass was restored in neighbouring parishes. A force was gathered and gaining strength as it marched, went to Crediton where it joined a Cornish force which had risen independently a few days earlier. The rebels

were soon in effective control of the west country and
could have reached London with competent leadership.
But they were not organized revolutionaries with an
objective and a strategy—they were humble men who
had risen spontaneously to defend the Faith of their
fathers.

The Protestant historian, Professor W. G. Hoskins, is
unable to conceal his admiration when describing their
march on Exeter. "With the sacred banner of the
Five Wounds of Christ floating before them, and the
pyx borne under a rich canopy, with crosses, banners,
candlesticks, swinging censers, and holy bread and
water 'to defend them from devils and the adverse
power,' the procession of Devon and Cornish farmers
and labourers, led by a few of the gentry, ignorantly
pitting themselves against the whole power of the State,
marched on to Exeter behind their robed priests, sing-
ing as they advanced; a pathetic, futile, and gallant
rebellion."[7] Futile? In worldly terms perhaps—but
sub specie aeternitatis . . . ?

"We do not know how many conservative and
stubborn West countrymen marched in that hopeless
rebellion: a few thousands probably. They spoke and
fought for tens of thousands, no doubt, who disliked
and detested the changes. But in most parishes the
parson and his people accepted the orders from above
and conformed outwardly."[8]

Even in Exeter the majority, including the mayor and
chief citizens, disliked the reforms, but as was the case
with Catholics throughout all the persecutions and penal
times, they faced an agonizing choice between the
dictates of religion and an obligation, which in itself
they regarded to be religious, of obedience to the
crown. The Protestant historian Hooker concedes that
the party " of the old stamp and of the Romish religion " was larger than the Protestant group in Exeter
but that " the magistrates and chieftains of the city
albeit they were not fully resolved and satisfied in
religion yet they not respecting that but chiefly their
dutifulness to the king and commonwealth, nothing
liked the rebellion . . ."[9]

So widespread was popular feeling in support of the rebels that even those who lacked the courage to join them were not willing to fight against them. Lord Russell, the Lord Privy Seal and an experienced soldier, had been sent to crush the rebellion. He found it almost impossible to raise local levies to combat the men of Devon and Cornwall, not simply in those counties but in Dorset, Wiltshire, and Somerset. The strong Catholic sympathies of the people of Somerset are made clear by a letter from the King's Council to Lord Russell suggesting a method of overcoming their reluctance: ". . . Where ye declare that thoccasyon of being able to levie so few in Somersetshire is the evil inclynation of the people, and that there are amongs them that do not styck openly to speak such traterous words agaynst the kyng and in favour of the traytrous rebels. Ye shall hang two or three of them, and cause them to be executed lyke traytors. And that wilbe the only and best staye of all those talks."[10]

Even Protestant historians concede that the Western Rebellion was genuinely religious.[11] The rebels were attacked by a propaganda campaign as well as with military forces. The government propagandists warned the West country men that they were deceived by their priests "whelps of the Romish litter".[12] It had, in fact, been the laity who had forced or shamed their priests into making a stand for the Faith. Nicholas Udall, a Protestant scholar who had gained the favour of Edward VI through the patronage of Catherine Parr, derided the rebels for their pronouncements against heresy which, he claimed, they did not understand. The changes were, he insisted, based on the "most godly council . . . with long study and travail of the best learned bishops and doctors of the realm."[13] Had the rebels had the learning or debating skill of St. Thomas More they could have pointed out that the traditional religion had the support of a numberless host of the best learned bishops and doctors, stretching back in time to the apostles themselves.

The religious nature of the rebellion is made clear

by the demands of the rebels. " Fyrst we wyll have
the general counsall and the holy decrees of our forefathers observed, kept and performed and who so ever
shal agayne saye them, we hold them as Heretikes
. . . we will have the masse in Latten, as before . . .
we will have the Sacrament hange over the hyeyhe
aulter, and there to be worshypped as it was wount
to be, and they whiche will not thereto consent, we
wyl have them dye lyke heretykes against the Holy
Catholyque fayth . . . we wyl have palmes and asshes
at the tymes accustomed, Images to be set up again
in every church, and all other auncient olde Cere-
monyes used heretofore, by our mother the holy
church . . . we wil not receyve the newe servye
because it is like a Christmas game, but we wyll have
oure old service of Mattens, masse, Evensong and procession in Latten not in English, as it was before."[14]

Like Nicholas Udall, Cranmer took great delight in
ridiculing the rebels for their ignorance. " When I
first read your request, O ignorant men of Devonshire
and Cornwall, straightways came to my mind a
request, which James and John made unto Christ ; to
whom Christ answered : ' You ask you wot not what.'
Even so thought I of you, as soon as ever I heard your
articles, that you were decived by some crafty priest,
which devised those articles for you, to make you ask
you wist not what."[15]   In his very lengthy reply to
the fifteen demands of the rebels he shows himself to
be as outraged by the manner in which the demands
are phrased as by the demands themselves. " Is this
the fashion of subject to speak unto their prince, ' We
will have '?   Was this manner of speech at any time
used of subjects to their prince since the beginning of
the world?   Have not all true subjects ever used to
their sovereign lord this form of speaking, ' Most
humbly beseecheth your faithful and obedient subject? '   Although the papists have abused your ignorance
in propounding such articles, which you understand
not, yet you should not have suffered yourselves to be
led by the nose and bridled by them, that you should
clearly forget your duty of allegiance unto your

sovereign lord, saying unto him, ' This we will have ' ;
and that saying with armour upon your backs and
swords in your hands."

Cranmer considered the plea for the return of Latin
particularly ridiculous. " For the whole that is done
should be the act of the people and pertain to the people,
as well as to the priest.[16]   And standeth it with reason,
that the priest should speak for you, and in your name,
and you answer him again in your own person ; yet
you understand never a word, neither what he saith,
nor what you say yourselves? . . . Had you rather be
like pies or parrots, that be taught to speak, and yet
understand not one word what they say, than be true
Christian men, that pray unto God in heart and in
faith?"

Cardinal Gasquet points out how mistaken is the
notion that the Latin service is a closed book to the
uneducated in Catholic countries.   " The Latin words
become not infrequently so familiar that they suggest
themselves to the uneducated even in the occurrences
of ordinary daily life.   Therefore in considering the
sudden substitution of English for Latin in all the
public services of the Church it must be borne in mind
that to a very great number this measure, so far from
affording any gratification to their religious feelings,
was one to which they had to be reconciled."[17]   The
Cardinal also quotes the opinion of an unprejudiced
Anglican scholar whose travels in Catholic countries
had convinced him that the ordinary faithful could
follow the audible parts of the Mass " quite as well as
the English generally follow the prayer book."[18]

The Western rebels had demanded that those who
refused their demands should " dye lyke heretykes
against the holy Catholyque fayth."   In the event, of
course, it was the rebels who died when the rebellion
was eventually crushed with the help of foreign mercenaries commanded by Lord Russell and Lord Grey de
Wilton who had joined him after putting down another
religious rising in Oxfordshire.   The only reliable troops
were the mercenaries, Italians, Spaniards, and Germans.
When they eventually discovered the religious nature of

the campaign in which they had fought, many of them sought absolution.[19] " There was a fierce battle at Clyst St. Mary and another at Clyst Heath, where the rebels died by hundreds ; and after the battle a massacre of the prisoners. And then in the night of August 4th and 5th the rebels withdrew from Exeter."[20] Lord Grey had never fought against Englishmen before and marvelled at " such stoutness . . . never in all the wars did he know the like ".[21]

The rebellion was far from over, however, and the final battle took place at Sampford Courtenay where the rebellion had begun. Groups of rebels still kept up the fight, retreating into Somerset and at least 4,000 west country men died at the hands of the royal army. Thomas Cranmer's Prayer Book had had its baptism of blood. " By the end of August it was all over," writes Professor Bindoff, ". . . some thousands of peasant households mourned their menfolk slaughtered on the battlefield, some hundreds those who expiated their treasons on the gallows of a dozen counties."[22]

Cardinal Gasquet writes: ". . . the imposition of the book of the new service was only effected through the slaughter of many thousands of Englishmen by the English government helped by their foreign mercenaries. The old dread days of the Pilgrimage of Grace were renewed, the same deceitful methods were employed to win success, the same ruthless bloodshed was allowed in the punishment of the vanquished. Terror was everywhere struck into the minds of the people by the sight of the executions, fixed for the market days, of priests dangling from the steeples of their parish churches, and of the heads of laymen set up in the high places of the towns."[23] The parish priest of the church of St. Thomas (Exeter) was hanged on a gallows erected on his church tower in his Mass vestments, with " a holy water bucket, a sprinkler, a sacring bell, a pair of beads and such other like popish trash hanged about him."[24]

The last act in the western tragedy was the execution of the leaders at Tyburn on 7th January, 1550. The very objective Venetian envoy reported that: " had the country people only a leader, although they had been grievously chastised they would rise again."[25] Thus were the peasants of the West induced to accept " the very godly order set forth by order of Parliament for common prayer in the mother tongue."

Bernadette Keenan's faithful drawing from a photograph of a carving of the Five Sacred Wounds in an oak bench-end at Lapford Church, North Devon, by kind permission of the rector. The carving is believed to be original pre-Reformation work

Chapter XV

" BELIEVE AS YOUR FOREFATHERS "

"Through the perverse obstinacy and dissembling forward-
ness of many of the inferior priests and ministers of the
Cathedrals and other churches of this realm, there did arise a
marvellous schism and variety of fashions in celebrating the
common service and administration of the sacraments and
other rites and ceremonies of the Church. For some, zealously
allowing the king's proceedings did gladly follow the order
thereof: and others, though not so willingly admitting them
yet dissembling and patchingly use some part of them; but
many carelessly contemning all, would still exercise their old
wonted popery."—Foxe: *Acts and Monuments*, V. 720.

THE WESTERN rebellion represented the most
dramatic and heroic reaction of the ordinary faithful to
the new prayer book. Those who fought and died for
the old Mass did so, as Professor Hoskins explains,
" for tens of thousands, no doubt, who disliked and
detested the changes ". Another Protestant historian,
Professor Owen Chadwick, concedes that even at the
end of Edward's brief reign: " The Reformation in
England had captured the genuine allegiance only of a
few instructed theologians and some educated merchants
and other members of the middle class, particularly in
London, and was supported for less unmixed motives by
noble potentates."[1] Bucer complained of those whose
support for the reforms was nothing but " the greed of
men to seize the wealth of the Church ".[2] There was
a good deal of money to be made out of the Reformation for those with the inclination and initiative to do
so!

Dr. John Ponet attacked opponents of the reform in
a sermon preached before the King and court in March,

1550. He complained of those who trod the most holy
word of God under their feet. " ' Believe ' say they ' as
your forefathers have done before you ' and in this mind
they counsel all men to stand and remain still stiffly
without searching any further." This, he complains,
would involve acceptance " of the popish mass and all
such trumpery." Dr. Ponet claims that these talks
have been sown abroad and bruited among the people
by " the judges in their circuits and the justices of peace
that be popishly affected, by bishops and their officers
in their synods and other meetings of ecclesiastical
persons, by schoolmasters in their grammar schools, by
stewards when they keep their courts, by priests when
they sit and hear auricular confession, and such like as
mind nothing else but the plain subversion of the
kingdom of Christ and all christian doctrine, and setting
up again the doctrine and kingdom of the Romish antichrist to God's great dishonour . . . The bishop and
his officers persuade the priests of the county that they
shall also follow ancient customs and usages in the
church, and believe and do as the church believeth and
hath taught them, meaning by the church the church
of Rome, though they say not so expressly." Dr. Ponet
is particularly severe on schoolmasters who " will pour
this talk into the ears of his scholars. Oh! what hurt
these popish schoolmasters do. They mar all, most
noble prince, poisoning the children's ears with popery
in their youth." He adds that the zeal of these popish
schoolmasters is such that whenever they discover that
the father of one of their pupils is a supporter of the
reforms the poor boy gets birched " thrice against his
fellows once."[3] An example, perhaps, of the biblical
adage regarding the sins of the fathers being visited
upon their children.

Another Protestant testimony to the lack of support
for the reforms comes from Bucer. It is interesting to
note his sound grasp of what would now be termed
the principles of religious sociology when he explains
the folly of imposing radical changes upon people who
do not understand them and have not been prepared for
them. In a letter to the King in 1551 he writes: " Your

Sacred Majesty has already found by experience how grave are the evils which ensued on taking away by force false worship from your people without sufficient preliminary instruction. The instruments of impiety have been snatched from them by proclamations and the observance of true religion has been imposed by royal command. Some have on this account made horrible sedition, others have raised perilous dissensions in the state, and to this very day wherever they can they either cause new trouble or increase what has already been excited. Some turn the prescribed form of service into a mere papistical abuse. Although it is now in the vulgar tongue, the ' sacrificers ' recite it of set purpose so indistinctly that it cannot be understood, whilst the people altogether refuse to understand or to listen. Not a few of the priests show forth the sacred communion of Christ as the papistical mass and the people are present with no other intention than to assist at the mass itself. Hardly anyone takes the Sacrament from the table of the Lord except the priest or the sexton, and even he does so unwillingly."[4]

The fact that the Reformers expected to encounter strong opposition is indicated by provisions in the Act of Uniformity prohibiting " any interludes, plays, songs, rhymes or any other open words in derogation, depraving or displaying of the same book (of Common Prayer) ; or of anything contained therein."[5]

Another testimony to the extent of conservative resistance comes from Peter Martyr. "Many things remain to be done which we have in expectation rather than reality. The perseverence of the bishops is incredible. They oppose us with all their might ; yet some of that order, although very few, are favourable to the undertaking.

" The labour of the most reverend the archbishop of Canterbury (Cranmer) is not to be expressed, for whatever has hitherto been wrested from them, we have acquired solely by the industry and activity and importunity of the prelate ; and this circumstance gives us encouragement, that some addition is always being made to what we have already obtained."[6]

The champions of the old Faith were well aware of the equivocal character of the new prayer book and were quick to point out its significant omissions— particularly " the omission of all sacrificial language."[7] The King's Council took immediate notice of this opposition and in doing so provided testimony of some of the forms it was taking.   Bonner, the very conservative Bishop of London, was a great thorn in the side of the Reformers.   He is often criticised for his implacability in the persecution of Protestants under Mary, but the humiliations and persecutions he endured during the reign of Edward VI should be taken into consideration. In a letter to Bonner dated 25th July, 1549, the King and Council complain that the new book " remaineth in many places of our realm either not known at all or not used," or that it is used " so that the people have not that spiritual delectation in the same that to good Christians appertaineth."[8]

On 10th August, 1549, Bonner was summoned before the Lords of the Council and handed certain injunctions for his future guidance.   Complaint is made " that divers of our city of London and other places within your diocese assemble themselves very seldom and fewer times than they were heretofore accustomed unto Common Prayer and to Holy Communion."   Further " that divers as well in London as in other parts of your diocese do frequent and haunt foreign rites and masses and contemn and forbear to praise God and pray for his majesty after such rites and ceremonies as in this realm are approved and set out by authority."[9]

Bonner took no heed of these warnings and on 13th September he was duly articled before the Ecclesiastical Commissioners on the information of Latimer and Hooper for " nonconformity ".[10]   One of the articles read as follows:

" Item, that ye know, or have heard say, that certain persons within your diocese, sith the time that the said Injunctions were given unto you, have heard, been at, or celebrate mass, or evensong in the Latin tongue, and after the old rite and manner, other than according to the King's majesty's book."[11]

Eventually, on 15th September, 1549, Bishop Bonner felt that his failure to make an explicit public protest against the reforms " might unto some be an allowance of heretical doctrines." He had been forced to allow a Protestant to preach in his own Cathedral of St. Paul and when, in his sermon, the preacher declaimed " against the Holy Sacrament, denying the verity and presence of Christ's true body and blood to be there " the bishop rose from his place and left the church.

Four days later he explained to Cranmer " three things I have, to wit, a small portion of goods, a poor carcass and mine soul: the first two ye may take (though unjustly) to you ; but as for my soul, ye get it not *quia anima in manibus meis semper.*"[12] That same night he was conveyed to the Marshalsea prison.[13]

" After the imposition of the ' new uniform order ' of worship in the summer of 1549, and the suppression of the popular risings, the pace of the Protestant movement quickened. An Act of Parliament, reinforced by a royal proclamation, ordered the calling in and destruction of all the old Mass books, which the recalcitrants continued to use ; the reforming bishops diligently searched out survivals of ' popish superstition ' in the liturgy ; churches were denuded of their vestments, and texts aimed against the Real Presence and the Mass were painted on the walls."[14] This phase of the Edwardian Reformation is described as " purely destructive " by the Protestant historian, Professor T. S. Bindoff: " It ordered the suppression of all servicebooks other than the Prayer Book and Henry VIII's Primer, and the destruction of all remaining religious statues and paintings. ' All books called antiphoners, missals scrayles, processionals, manuals, legends, pyes, portuyses, primers in Latin or English, cowchers, journals ' so ran the catalogue of these fine flowers of medieval Faith and medieval art which were to be ' abolished, extinguished and forbidden for ever ' in favour of the austerity of the printed Book of Common Prayer. And in the frenzy of destruction which followed there perished much more than was warranted even by this comprehensive schedule. At Oxford the

Vice-Chancellor, Richard Cox, earned the sobriquet of the ' Cancellor ' for his zeal in prescribing, with the condemned liturgies, priceless books and manuscripts whose only taint of ' superstition ' was their red lettered or geometrical embellishments."[15]

Bucer has already been cited in this chapter as complaining of the manner in which the conservative clergy celebrated the new Communion service as if it had been a Mass. The most Protestant of the Edwardine bishops, Hooper, expressed his indignation at this practice in a letter to his friend Bullinger. He complained that although " the altars are here in many churches changed into tables the public celebration of the Lord's Supper is very far from the order and institution of Our Lord. Although it is administered in both kinds, yet in some places the Supper is celebrated three times a day. Where they used heretofore to celebrate in the morning the *mass* of the apostles, they now have the communion of the apostles . . . where they had the principal or high mass they now have, as they call it, the high communion. They still retain their vestments and the candles before the altars ; in the churches they always chant the hours and other hymns relating to the Lord's Supper, but in our own language. And that popery may not be lost, the mass-priests, although they are compelled to discontinue the use of the Latin tongue, yet most carefully observe the same tone and manner of chanting to which they were heretofore accustomed in the papacy."[16]

" Not merely was the communion celebration like the Mass in outward appearance, but the ancient Mass itself continued to be said by priests in secret. Bernard Gilpin, a grandnephew of Bishop Tunstall, even at the close of Edward's reign, and whilst holding the king's licence as a general preacher of the reformed doctrine, still ' at some times read mass ; but seldom and privately.' If this was the practice of one who was attached to the party of the innovators, the same must certainly have been the case with many who were zealous for the old doctrines."[17]   Professor Bindoff notes that soon after Mary's accession to the throne "the Mass was being celebrated in London churches 'not by commandment but of the people's devotion', and news was coming in of its unopposed revival throughout the country."[18]

The true feelings of the ordinary clergy, as opposed to the manner in which for a mixture of motives they decided to act, is well expressed in the history of one of their number given by Professor W. G. Hoskins. He shows how the religious changes are reflected in the parish accounts of Morebath, Devon, where Christopher Trychay was vicar from 1520-1573. "We see how the Reformation affected this parish uncomplicated by any change of parson, of new men coming in with new ideas. We find him buying a new suit of black (requiem) vestments at Exeter, where they were blessed, some time in 1547, bought partly from the small gifts of his parishioners, and giving thanks to them and to God: no inkling of the changes about to break over them. The high cross was gilded at the same time and the images cleaned. Then, at the end of the 1547 account— we read of three men and 'the high Wardens' riding to Tiverton to meet the king's commissioners, 'to make an answer for chantry ground.' In 1548 the vestments are put away, not sold or destroyed, but distributed among the principal farmers of the parish for safe keeping. The 'boke or erassamus' is bought, and the 'furst communion boke' in 1549. There is a good deal of riding to Tiverton and to Exeter 'to answer for maters concernyng ye kyng'.

"In 1551 John Lowsmpre is paid three shillings for taking away the side altars and rood loft, the gold in the church images is sold to a brazier of Exeter. Then comes the blessed relief of Mary's reign: the vestments are returned from the farmhouse to the church, the images are brought out from their hiding places, and the vicar—who had allowed no word of regret to creep into his accounts as he detailed the stripping of his church year after year—now speaks from his heart at the restoration of the Catholic Faith: 'Item of John Williams of Bery we received again an image of Mary and the king and queen concerning St. George. And of William Morsse at Lauton was received an image of John. And of the widow Jurdyn trails and knots. And of divers other persons here was rescued pageants and books and divers other things concerning our rood-loft. Like true and faithful Christian people this was restored to this church, by which doings it showeth they did like good Catholic men.'

" This was in 1555. In the following year the side altar dedicated to St. Sidwell was replaced, and the rood loft put up again. Then, in 1562 it all goes again, and throughout the rest of the 1560's and 1570's we see the small changes taking place that were to produce the Church of England: the commandments put up on either side of the altar in 1568, the reference to the communion table in 1570—no longer the high altar with its gilded cross and the pyx hanging over it—the buying of Dr. Jewel's book, the English translation of his *Apologia pro Ecclesia Anglicana,* at Exeter, and of a chain for it. The old vicar still dozed in the vicarage, and pottered along to the church to perform his duties, but he was the only thing that had not changed during the half century. It is idle to speculate on what he thought in his old age."[19]

" Clergy who refused to use the book of 1549, criticised it, or used any other (even in private chapels), were to lose a year's income and be imprisoned for six months; on a second conviction to lose their benefices and to go prison for a year; on a third, to be imprisoned for life. For laymen who criticised, or caused other rites to be celebrated or hindered the new, there were also fines and imprisonment: £10 or three months on a first conviction; £20 or six months on a second; loss of all goods and life imprisonment on a third. The new Act of 1552 began by lamenting that, notwithstanding 'the very godly order set forth by the authority of Parliament for common prayer in the mother tongue,' something 'very comfortable to all good people' desiring to live a Christian life, 'a great number of people in divers parts of this realm . . . refuse to come to their parish churches and other places where common prayer . . . is used '. So failure to attend the services on Sundays and holy days, 'there to abide orderly and soberly during the time of the common prayer' was now made an offence, which the bishops were authorised to punish with such censures as excommunication, according to 'the king's ecclesiastical laws'; while the penalties of 1549 apply now to the book of 1552, described as the older book 'explained and made fully perfect'. Moreover, a new offence is created: anyone who is present at services of prayer, 'administration of sacraments, making of ministers in the churches' or any rite at all otherwise done than is set forth in the Prayer Book, shall upon conviction go to prison for six months on the first offence, for a year on the second, and for life on the third.

"Such are the first penalties to be enacted in England for the new crime of hearing Mass, or of receiving the sacraments *as they had been received ever since St. Augustine came to convert the English, nearly a thousand years before.*"[20]

Mgr. Hughes' assessment of the religious state of England at the beginning of the reign of Edward VI was cited at the beginning of Chapter XI. The significance of the religious changes of his reign are explained by Professor Chadwick: " Under the Duke of Northumberland as Protector, the English reforming party succeeded between 1550 and 1553 in doing all that a German or Swiss city had done. They produced a new and simplified liturgy in the vernacular, with a Swiss doctrine of the eucharist, published a new statement of doctrine conforming at least in outline to the pattern of Swiss theology (The Forty-Two Articles of 1553), stripped the churches of images and side altars, replaced the high altar with a holy table, forbade the use of ceremonies other than those expressly provided in the Prayer Book ; and appropriated to secular use a proportion of church property. They weakened the authority of the bishops, by extending the policy of Henry VIII to replace it by a direct exercise of the royal supremacy. Where the bishops refused to accompany the reform, they were removed from their sees— Bonner of London, Gardiner of Winchester, Tunstall of

Durham, Day of Chichester, Heath of Worcester—and replaced."[21]

The general effect of the religious upheaval upon the life of the nation was a deplorable decline in the nation's manners and morals. Some Protestants would prefer to consider this as a legacy from the past but, as an outstanding historian of Tudor England, Professor S. T. Bindoff, explains ". . . the facts themselves are indisputable. Wherever we look, from the Royal Court and the circles of government down to the villages and parish, and whatever type of evidence we choose, from Latimer's sweeping denunciations to the detailed facts and figures yielded by the records of royal and diocesan visitations, we are confronted by the same black picture of irreligion, irreverence and immorality on a terrifying scale."[22]

A plaque on the wall of the Church of the Sacred Heart and St. Ia at St. Ives, Cornwall, in memory of John Payne, portreeve, who was hanged in the market place, and all the men of St. Ives who died to defend the Catholic Faith in the Western Rising

Chapter XVI

THE PATTERN OF COMPROMISE

"There be certain thought to have Masses in their houses, which come very seldom or not at all to church . . . which keep, as it were, schools in their houses of Popery, deriding and mocking this religion and the Ministers thereof, which be a marvellous stumbling to the Queen's Majesty's loving subjects in this country . . . I confess that I am not able to reform these, except I should be mightily backed by your honourable authority."

The Bishop of Hereford to the Privy Council, 1564

IT HAS been shown in previous chapters that most of the Catholic minded clergy preferred to interpret Cranmer's Communion Service in an orthodox manner rather than offer any open resistance. Christopher Trychay of Morebath, described in Chapter XV, is a typical example. It would, of course, be very wrong to pass any judgement on such priests. It is easy to be wise with hindsight. " No compromise!" sounds well as a slogan, but how many Catholics today can honestly say that they would *certainly* have acted differently? It is for God to judge them and we are assured that He is merciful. While it would be wrong to pass judgements on those who compromised, it is quite legitimate to comment on the pattern of compromise itself, and its consequences.

Martyrs are, of course, the exception rather than the rule. But another factor must have weighed heavily with the Edwardian clergy—*that of obedience to lawfully constituted authority.* The will of the king was considered to be the Will of God—scholars like St. Thomas More could make a vital distinction between the duties owed to Caesar and the duties owed to God. Such a distinction did not seem so clear to ordinary parochial

clergy. The 1549 Prayer Book appeared to be imposed
legally. Open resistance would be an act of rebellion
and divide the nation. Cardinal Gasquet comments:
" In Edward's reign the outcome of such principles was
to induce those who held a public position to put the
best interpretation possible upon every measure, however much they may have resisted its imposition and
disliked its object."[1] Compromise on a matter of
principle is always a mistake. Bishops and priests
like Gardiner had, of course, already abandoned
their Catholicism by accepting the royal supremacy.
To be a Catholic it is essential to be in communion with the Holy See. Once one compromise has
been made the next is easier—for any compromise
on a matter of principle involves a degree of deception,
if only self-deception, and once entered into this
becomes a self-perpetuating process. Catholic historians and bishops cited in this study condemn the
new communion service as unacceptable because of the
serious omissions from the traditional Mass. The
omissions were designed to make it possible to interpret
the new rite in a manner consonant with a denial of
Catholic teaching on the sacrifice and the Real
Presence. The fact that it did not contain formal heresy
or explicit denials of Catholic doctrine is considered to
be irrelevant. What is not affirmed is considered to be
denied. Gardiner must certainly have realised this
clearly, and, in a criticism of him, Fr. Messenger makes
a criticism of all the compromising clergy who fell into
the trap laid for them by the Reformers. " In order to
approve the Book of Common Prayer, he attributed to
it the orthodox Catholic doctrine on the Real Presence,
on the strength of a few ambiguous phrases, to which
we have already alluded. He ignored the passages
which point clearly in an opposite direction."[2]

The fact that mutilations and excisions are doctrinally
of greater significance than the mere absence in a rite
of any clear expression of doctrine has been recognised
even by the Anglican *Church Times.* It commented
apropos of Anglican Orders: " It is true that the
Anglican Reformers were not only silent in the Ordinal

as to any intention to confer the power of sacrifice, but they actually cut out the reference to sacrifice which the older formula contained. *To cut out is a more significant action than to refrain from putting in.*"[3]

When the 1552 Prayer Book was imposed it was quite impossible to interpret it in anything but a Protestant sense. Professor Bindoff writes: " The most important changes were again those concerning the Eucharist. No longer was it possible for conservative minds to give the communion service that Catholic interpretation which had reconciled Gardiner and others to it in 1549. Communion was now to be celebrated at a table, not an altar ; ordinary bread was to be used, and any left over was to be consumed by the curate ; the celebrant was no longer to wear special vestments nor make devotional gestures ; and the order of service was changed so as to block the last loophole through which anyone might glimpse the forbidden vision of sacrifice."[4]

But the pattern of compromise had established itself so completely that acceptance of the 1552 Prayer Book was virtually universal. Priests who had accepted the introduction of English into the liturgy in 1547 ; of new elements into the traditional Mass in 1548 ; and the ambiguous service of 1549, were inclined to say " It's too late now " rather than " Enough is enough " or " Thus far and no farther."

This pattern of compromise had reached the point that by 1559, after a reversion to Protestantism under Elizabeth following the brief return to the Church under Mary, the parochial clergy as a whole made no open resistance to the change. At least " three-fourths of these priests now abandoned both the Mass and the Pope as easily as priests of twenty-five years earlier had abandoned the Roman Supremacy alone."[5]

In fairness to the bishops, it must be pointed out that only two of the seventeen Marian bishops retained their sees under Elizabeth (those of Llandaff and of Sodor and Man). Fourteen bishops, twelve deans, fifteen heads of colleges, and between two and three hundred clergy resigned their offices or were deprived.[6] " The very idea of an actual sacrifice disappeared as utterly, wherever the new Christianity triumphed, as did that other idea that the Church of Christ is founded to be man's infallible teacher. What was left, as the sacrament of the Lord's Supper, was a devotional exercise preparatory to the faithful man's receiving the holy tokens which commemorated Our Lord's sacrificial offering of Himself for us upon the Cross—and in the moment when the faithful man so received this consecrated bread and wine, Christ was mysteriously received by him in his heart, 'only after an heavenly and spiritual manner'.

" It is still hard for a Catholic to grasp the fact that these theories and rites were, in a very great measure at least, the accomplishment of men who were priests, who had not only received the Catholic sacraments, but had said Mass ; and who had now come to be satisfied with this, and without any sign of regret that the old could not be.

" One thing was immediately evident—that in the new religion the collective piety of the Church was not to be dominated by the Lord's Supper as the collective life of Catholicism has, from the beginning, been dominated by the Mass . . . In the eyes of the Reformers their new rite never had the importance which the Mass always held for the Catholic. It could never have been said ' It's the Lord's Supper that matters '—and had it been said, in the sense of the classic saying about the Mass so familiar to us all, the Reformers would have been the first to deny the saying. And as they knew so well the nature of what they had devised, they knew also the power of what they had rejected. In one sense they still paid more attention to the Mass than to their own eucharistic rites for against the Mass itself they never ceased to wage war ; and all through these first generations of the Reform the flood of bitter, lying— and even indecent propaganda against it, and against the doctrine of the Real Presence, never ceased. None were more zealous in opposing the changes of 1559, said Jewel, than those won back to Catholicism in Mary's reign: *Tanti est semel gustasse de missa;* and to attack the Mass immediately was, therefore, the best strategy of all. *Vident erepto illo palladio omnia ventura in periculum* ('This it is to have once tasted the Mass.' 'They perceive that when that palladium is removed, everything else will be endangered ')."[7]

There were, of course, those who refused to compromise. Professor Chadwick explains: " A small number were not reconciled to change and preferred to maintain their traditional worship in other lands. These men were not attracted by the whitewash and the destruction or by seeing vestments, pyxes, images, copes, altars and censers being sold on the open market."[8] Above all, it was the young men who went to seminaries in Europe who preserved the Faith in Britain. They returned to give the Mass to the people and only too often their lives for the Mass, the traditional Latin Mass which is found in the Missal of St. Pius V.[9]

Cardinal Newman remarks in one of his most celebrated sermons, *The Second Spring,* that it was " the high decree of heaven, that the majesty of Catholicism should be blotted out " in Britain. " So all seemed to be lost ; and there was a struggle for a time and then its priests were cast out or martyred. There were sacrileges innumerable. Its temples were profaned or destroyed ; its revenues seized by covetous nobles, or squandered upon the ministers of the new faith. The presence of Catholicism was at length removed,—its grace disowned,—its power despised,—its name, except as a matter of history, at length almost unknown . . . No longer the Catholic Church in the country ; nay, no longer, I may say, a Catholic community,—but a few adherents of the Old Religion, moving silently and sorrowfully about, as memorials of what had been. 'The Roman Catholics ; '—not a sect, not even an interest, as men conceived it . . . but merely a handful of individuals, who might be counted, like the pebbles and *detritus* of the great deluge . . . found in corners, and alleys, and cellars, and the housetops, or in the recesses of the country ; cut off from the populous world around them, and dimly seen, as if through a mist or in twilight, as ghosts flitting to and fro, by the high Protestants, the lords of the earth."

But this despised remnant had a treasure denied to those who treated them with such contempt, the Mass of St. Pius V, "the most beautiful thing this side of heaven". This was the pearl of great price for which they were prepared to pay all that they had,—and pay it they did, priest and layman, butcher's wife and schoolmaster. The victors had the churches and cathedrals built for the celebration of the traditional Latin Mass, the vanquished had the Mass, and it was the Mass that mattered.

> "Blessed are they that suffer persecution for justice's sake for theirs is the kingdom of heaven."—(Matt. 5:10)

Appendix I

THE OPUS OPERATUM

The sacramental system, the *opus operatum,* imparts grace directly from God. The sacraments themselves are the source of the grace they convey providing they are administered by an authorised minister who intends to do what the Church intends and observes the correct ritual. This automatic transmission of grace by a correctly administered sacrament is referred to as grace received *ex opere operato.* It is made possible because Christ Himself is the true minister of all the sacraments, the human ministers only acting as His instruments. We receive the grace of the sacraments directly from Christ no matter how unworthy the intermediary. It would, of course, be a grave sin on the part of the minister to administer a sacrament while conscious of unabsolved mortal sin, indeed it would be a sacrilege. But if, for example, a priest offered Mass or heard confessions while in a state of mortal sin this would not prevent the faithful receiving the sacramental grace which comes to them from Christ.

Although the grace of the sacraments is made available automatically, *ex opere operato,* its fruitfulness in those who have reached the age of reason is affected to some extent by their dispositions. As we are told in the *Lauda Sion,* the sequence for *Corpus Christi,* the same sacrament can have the opposite effect, life for some and death for others. This is the teaching of St. Paul: "For he that eateth and drinketh unworthily, eateth and drinketh judgement to himself, not discerning the body of the Lord". (1 Cor. 11:29)

The influence of the dispositions of the recipient upon the fruits of the sacrament is referred to as *ex opere*

operantis. It is of the very greatest importance to stress
that in no way at all is the grace of a sacrament ever
produced *ex opere operantis,* the dispositions of the
recipient can only help to determine its effectiveness,
they are never the cause or source of grace, which only
comes from Christ Himself.

Because the Church is nothing less than the extension of the Incarnation throughout the ages and
throughout the nations, because the Church is Christ
saving and sanctifying His elect, it is clear that the
Mystical Body is to be the normal channel of grace,
above all through the seven sacraments. It is, however, important to realise that God is not bound by the
sacramental system even though He instituted it, and
that He can and does give grace in other ways to those
who do not have access to the sacraments and who have
never had the saving word of faith proclaimed to them.
" Is a man in Persia acceptable to God?" asks St. John
Chrysostom. " If he is worthy, then he is acceptable
by being found worthy of the Faith. That is why the
Ethiopian eunuch was acceptable and was not overlooked. But what about the good men who *are* overlooked? Out upon you ; no man is overlooked if he
be devout." (PG 60: 178).

The axiom " outside the Church there is no salvation "
was well explained by Cardinal Bourne in his introduction to the Catholic Truth Society edition of Pope Pius
XI's Encyclical on *True Religious Unity* (*Mortalium
Animos*). While this axiom is perfectly true, the
Cardinal explains, " it is equally true that without the
deliberate act of the will there can be neither fault nor
sin, so evidently this axiom applies only to those who
are outside the Church knowingly, deliberately and
wilfully.

" And this is the doctrine of the Catholic Church on
this often misunderstood and misrepresented aphorism.
There are the covenanted and the uncovenanted dealings
of God with His creatures, and no creature is outside
His fatherly care. There are millions—even at this day
the vast majority of mankind—who are still unreached
or unaffected by the message of Christianity in any

shape or form. There are large numbers who are persuaded that the old covenant still prevails and are perfectly sincere and conscientious in their observance of the Jewish law. And there are millions who accept some form of Christian teaching who have never adverted to the idea of Unity as I have described it, and have no thought that they are obliged in conscience to accept the teaching and to submit to the authority of the Catholic Church. All such, whether separated wholly from acceptance of Christ and His teaching or accepting that teaching only to the extent to which they have perceived it, will be judged on their own merits. They are bound to accept and follow God's teaching so far as their reason rightly used shall lead them. They must obey the dictates of the moral law which their conscience imposes upon them. They must regret before God, and endeavour to undo, the faults and sins that they commit against their reason and their conscience. And they are bound at all cost to enter within the Unity of the Church as soon as they realise that that obligation is incumbent upon them."

Appendix II

ARTICLE THIRTY-ONE

The Anglo-Catholic movement in the nineteenth century wished to restore Catholic belief and practice to the Church of England but found the Thirty-nine Articles, particularly the Thirty-first, a great hindrance in attaining this objective. An evangelical historian, J. T. Tomlinson, rightly comments: "The stern and uncompromising language of our Thirty-first Article has always been a thorn in the side of the Romanisers." He adds that despite their "solemn functions and gorgeous pageantry, they seem never able to quite shake off the consciousness that the Church to which their allegiance has been pledged, has pronounced the whole thing a 'blasphemous fable and a dangerous deceit'."[1] In his study of English Canon Law, E. Garth Moore stresses the fact that: "It is essential to remember that they (the Thirty-nine Articles) require the strictest literal interpretation. It is essential to remember that they must be read together with His Majesty's Declaration, which forms the preface to them and which states explicitly, '. . . no man hereafter shall either print, or preach, to draw the Article aside in any way, but shall submit to it in the plain and full meaning thereof: and shall not put his own sense or comment to the meaning of the Article, but shall take it in the literal and grammatical sense'."[2]

The most celebrated attempt to interpret Article XXXI contrary to the "plain and full meaning thereof" was made in Newman's Tract 90. J. T. Tomlinson rightly asks how such a non-natural interpretation "could have satisfied any candid mind".[3] However, a man of Newman's scholarship and integrity was in-

capable of maintaining such an untenable position and
eventually conceded that: "I do not see how it can
be denied that this Article calls the sacrifice of the
Mass itself . . . in all its daily celebrations from year's
end to year's end, *toto orbe terrarum,* a blasphemous
fable."[4]

It is unnecessary to discuss the interpretation of
Article XXXI in any detail as this has been done
authoritatively and exhaustively by Francis Clark in
Eucharistic Sacrifice and the Reformation. He pays
particular attention to the theory that the Reformers
did not reject the doctrine of the Eucharist as set out
by the Council of Trent but a varied assortment or
"errors" current in the sixteenth century. Francis
Clark documents the history of the alleged errors in
painstaking detail and demonstrates that almost invariably they have no factual basis. He makes it clear, as
this book should also do, that the Reformers understood
the Catholic teaching clearly and rejected it totally.
Nor was there any difference in the Eucharistic theology
of Trent and that of such a pre-Tridentine bishop as
St. John Fisher who faithfully reflected the accepted
consensus not only of the English but of the European
clergy. There were, of course, abuses connected with
the Mass—there was cupidity on the part of many
clerics and a "penny in the slot" attitude among many
of the faithful. But it was the theology of the Mass
which the Reformers rejected, they did not wish to
abolish incidental abuses but the sacrifice of the Mass
itself. This judgement finds ample support among
Anglican historians. Arguing from an Anglo-Catholic
standpoint in 1847, Nicholas Pocock called for the
abolition of the Articles and rightly insisted that to
argue that the Reformers only rejected pre-Reformation
errors was inconsistent with their known views.[5]
Writing from an Evangelical standpoint in 1962, the
Reverend Thomas Hewitt emphasises that it is "impossible to hold the strange theory that what the Reformers
meant to oppose in Article 31 was not the sacrifice of
the Mass as put forward by the Council of Trent, but
popular errors and abuses of the late mediaeval age,

and that a less crude doctrine of the Mass-sacrifice would have been acceptable to them ".[6]

As regards the attitude of the Reformers to the Council of Trent, it is of the greatest significance that when this Council in the Fourth Canon of its Twenty-Second Session anathematised those who stated that " the sacrifice of the Mass constitutes a blasphemy to the sacred sacrifice that Christ offered on the Cross ", the wording of Article XXXI was changed from its original form in which " the sacrifices of masses " were condemned as " forged fables, and daungerouse deceiptes " to its present wording of " blasphemous fables and dangerous deceits ". There are other examples of changes in the wording of the Articles to emphasise the fact that the Reformers rejected the teaching of Trent.[7] J. T. Tomlinson insists that the doctrine which the Reformers refused to accept (in his view, rightly) was: " this notion that priestly presentation on an altar on earth is the Divine method for communicating the benefits of the Cross. That was the evil which the English Reformers set themselves to combat, and which the Council of Trent tried to bolster up."[8]

Another straw at which some Anglo-Catholics grasped, including Newman, was the absurd idea that some special significance lies in the fact that Article XXXI refers to " sacrifices " in the plural rather than " sacrifice " in the singular. Both Tomlinson and Clark, from their divergent standpoints, show this to be completely nonsensical, as Newman eventually conceded. It is interesting to note that the term " sacrifices of Masses " is found in the various pre-Reformation English ordinals and was used by the Council of Florence.[9]

Francis Clark rightly points out that " the interpretation of the Reformers' attitude to the Mass does not depend upon one phrase in one document. They made their meaning clear not once but many times, by words, by writings, by official acts. Both in the singular and in the plural they referred to and rejected the same thing."[10]

It may appear unnecessary to devote so much attention to a theory which, if it ever had any credibility, lost it all after the appearance of *Eucharistic Sacrifice and the Reformation.* However, these discredited theories have been resurrected once again by Catholic ecumenists, particularly to justify the Agreed Statements on the Eucharist and Ministry (sic) issued by the Anglican/ Roman Catholic International Commission in 1971 and 1973. I have been present personally at a lecture during which a Catholic member of the Commission put forward the theory that the Anglican Reformers had not rejected the Mass but only late mediaeval abuses. In the Scottish Agreed Statement (drawn up by Catholics and Episcopalians in 1973) it is claimed that what is repudiated in Article XXXI " is something that never had been part of the teaching of the Roman Church ".[11] In Footnote 7 it actually tries to explain away the Article because it speaks of " sacrifices " in the plural and not " sacrifice " in the singular.[12]

Apart from anything else, to claim that Cranmer and his associates did not reject Catholic teaching on the Mass is a grave injustice to them. Whatever Catholics may think of Cranmer and the other Reformers, however much we may deplore their heretical beliefs and their hatred of the Church, we are bound to admit that many of them witnessed to the sincerity of their heretical Eucharistic belief by dying for it. To claim that their belief regarding the Mass was that of the Council of Trent is to make a mockery of their beliefs, their sincerity, and their courage.

NOTES

1. *The Prayer Book, Articles, and Homilies* (London, 1897), p. 284.
2. *An Introduction to English Canon Law* (Oxford, 1967), p. 55.
3. Op. cit., Note 1, p. 285.
4. *Via Media,* vol. II (London, 1901 edition), p. 316.
5. ESR, p. 34.
6. J. I. Packer (ed.), *Eucharistic Sacrifice* (London, 1962), p. 114.

7. See Chapter XII.
8. Op. cit., Note 1, p. 306.
9. D, 693.
10. ESR, p. 216.
11. *The Ecclesial Nature of the Eucharist* (Glasgow, 1973), p. 13.
12. Ibid., p. 27.

The most complete study of the question of Article XXXI can be found in *Eucharistic Sacrifice and the Reformation*. The books referred to in Notes 1 and 6 could also be consulted.

Appendix III

CHANGES IN THE WORDS OF CONSECRATION

Sarum Missal
WHO ON THE DAY
BEFORE HE SUFFERED
TOOK BREAD
INTO HIS HOLY AND
VENERABLE HANDS,
AND WITH HIS EYES
LIFTED
UP TO HEAVEN,
UNTO THEE GOD, HIS
FATHER ALMIGHTY,
GIVING THANKS TO
THEE, HE BLESSED,

BROKE,
AND GAVE IT TO HIS
DISCIPLES SAYING:
TAKE AND EAT YE
ALL OF THIS,
FOR THIS IS MY BODY.

IN LIKE MANNER,
AFTER HE HAD
SUPPED,
TAKING ALSO THIS
EXCELLENT
CHALICE
INTO HIS HOLY AND

1549 Prayer Book
Who in the same nyght
that he was betrayed:
tooke breade,

and when he had (blessed
and*) geuen thankes:
he brake it,
and gaue it
to his disciples, saiying:
Take, eate,

this is my bodye
which is geuen for you,
do this
in remembraunce of me.
Likewyse
after
supper
he toke

the cuppe,

VENERABLE HANDS,	
AND GIVING	and when he had
THANKS TO THEE	geuen thankes,
HE BLESSED	
AND GAVE TO HIS	he gaue it
DISCIPLES, SAYING:	to them, saiying:
TAKE	
AND DRINK	drynk
YE ALL OF THIS	ye all of this,
FOR THIS	for this
IS THE CHALICE	
OF MY BLOOD,	is my bloude
OF THE	of the
NEW AND ETERNAL	newe
TESTAMENT:	Testament,
THE	
MYSTERY OF FAITH:	
WHICH SHALL	whyche
BE SHED	is shed
FOR YOU	for you
AND FOR MANY	and for many,
UNTO THE	for
REMISSION OF	remission of
SINS.	synnes:

*"Blessed and" was omitted
in the 1552 Prayer Book.

BIBLIOGRAPHY

Some of the books referred to in the notes have been abbreviated as follows:

CCT   *Catechism of the Council of Trent,* translated by McHugh and Callan (New York), 1934.

CDT   *A Catholic Dictionary of Theology,* ed. J. Crehan, S.J. (London, 1962).

CT   *The Church Teaches* (Documents of the Church in English Translation), translated by J. F. Clarkson and others (Rockford, Illinois, 1973). This is an English version of the Denzinger *Enchiridion Symbolorum* and references to Denzinger in the notes, indicated by "D", can be located in this book.

CTD   *Concise Theological Dictionary,* Rahner & Vorgrimler (London, 1965).

CW   *The Works of Thomas Cranmer* (two vols.), Parker Society.

D   See: CT above.

DCD   *Development of Christian Doctrine,* J. H. Newman.

DEV   *Devon,* W. G. Hoskins (Newton Abbot, Devon, 1972).

EBCP   *Edward VI and the Book of Common Prayer,* Gasquet & Bishop (London, 1890). In the interests of brevity, only the first of the authors is mentioned when reference is made to this book.

ESR   *Eucharistic Sacrifice and the Reformation,* F. Clark (Oxford, 1967).

FSPB   *The First and Second Prayer Books of King Edward VI,* D. Harrison (Dean of Bristol) (London, 1968).

PHR   *The Reformation — A Popular History,* P. Hughes (London, 1960).

PS   Parker Society.

RIE   *The Reformation in England*, P. Hughes (three vols.) (London, 1950).

RMP   *The Reformation, The Mass, and the Priesthood*, E. C. Messenger (two vols.) (London, 1936).

RS   *The Recovery of the Sacred*, J. Hitchcock (New York, 1974).

TCC   *The Teaching of the Catholic Church*, G. Smith (London, 1956).

TE   *Tudor England*, S. T. Bindoff (London, 1952).

TM   *The Mass, A Study of the Roman Liturgy*, A. Fortescue (London, 1917).

TR   *The Reformation*, O. Chadwick (London, 1972).

TUD   *Tudor Rebellions*, A. Fletcher (London, 1973).

VAC   *A Vindication of the Bull 'Apostolicae Curae'*, The Cardinal Archbishop and Bishops of the Province of Westminster (London, 1898).

NOTES

CHAPTER I
1. DCD, Ch. I, Sect. I, 3.
2. *Roman Breviary*, Feast of the Annunciation, II Nocturn, Lesson vi.
3. *The Liturgical Year*, trans. Dom Laurence Shepherd (Dublin, 1968), vol. I, p. 7.
4. DCD, Ch. II, Sect. III, 2.
5. CDT, see entries: *Atonement, Redemption and Satisfaction*.
6. ST, III, Q. XLVIII, art II.
7. ESR, p. 554.
8. The various theories are summarised in the CDT entry: Atonement.
9. Commentary on Isaias 53.5.10; cited in ESR, p. 109.
10. ESR, p. 109, 110.
11. CTD, see entry *Satisfaction*.
12. *De erroribus Abaelardi*, no 21 (P.L. CLXXXII, col. 1070).
13. CCT, p. 227.
14. The most comprehensive history of the Reformation in Britain is the three volume study by Mgr. Philip Hughes (RIE). The author makes no attempt to hide the serious short-comings in the state of the Church but shows clearly that the Protestant Reformation was concerned essentially with doctrinal issues.
15. Encyclical Letter, *The Mystical Body of Jesus Christ* (C.T.S., London), p. 27.
16. ESR, p. 103; TCC, p. 693.
17. ESR, p. 103.

CHAPTER II
1. Lectures on Justification, 112.
2. D, 799.
3. Ibid.
4. ST, I-II, Q. CXIII, art. 9, ad. 2.
5. D, 797.
6. D, 798.
7. Ibid.
8. D, 809.
9. D, 810.
10. *Roman Breviary*, 2nd Nocturn, Lesson vi, Christ-mas Day.
For a detailed treatment of Justification and Grace see: ESR, Chapter VI.
CDT, Entries on Justification, Grace, Merit.
TCC, Chapters XVI and XVII.
CT, *Decree of Justification* of the Council of Trent, p. 230 ff.
Pius Parsch, *Seasons of Grace* (London, 1963). This is an invaluable exposition of the nature of grace as taught through the readings at Mass during the liturgical year. Much of this chapter is based upon Fr. Parsch's book.
D. Knowles, *Grace, The Life of the Soul*, C.T.S.

CHAPTER III
1. TR, 137.
2. Ibid., p. 144.
3. "It can hardly be pretended that in this matter of justification Cranmer has anything new to say. All his main points can be paralleled in Luther and Zwingli before him as well as Calvin and other contemporary writers. But what he does say he says clearly and forcibly, showing a fine grasp of the essentials of the Reformation position." G. W. Bromiley, *Thomas Cranmer Theologian*, p. 36. See also: ESR, pp. 139-144.
4. *Institutes of the Christian Religion*, Book II, chap. 16, nn. 2, 5.
5. CW, vol. I, p. 47.
6. CDT, vol. III, p. 180.
7. RIE, vol. I, p. 142.
8. Ibid.
9. H. Rondet, *The Grace of Christ* (Newman Press, 1967), page 279.
10. ESR, p. 143.
11. Cited in ESR, p. 364.
12. TCC, p. 763.
13. RIE, vol. II, p. 83.
14. ESR, p. 107.
15. ESR, p. 340.
16. John Bale, *Edwardine Bishop of Ossory, Select Works*, P.S., p. 153.
17. John Bradford (Chaplain to Bishop Ridley), *Letters, Treatises, Remains*, P.S., p. 270.

CHAPTER IV
1. De officiis ministrorum, lib. 1, cap. 48 (P.L. XVI, col. 101).
2. ST, III, Q.LXV, Art. III.
3. ST, III, Q.LXXXIII, Art. I.

4. Epistle LXIII, n. 17; (P.L. IV, col. 388-9).
5. TCC, p. 840.
6. Ibid.
7. Ibid, p. 839.
8. *Letter to the Bishops of Scotland*, 1898.
9. *The Mass of the Roman Rite* (London, 1959), p. 135.
10. Encyclical Letter, *Mediator Dei* (C.T.S., London), pp. 42-44.
11. *City of God*, Bk. X, chap. xx.
12. Pohle-Preuss, *The Sacraments* (London, 1916), vol. II, p. 388. M. de la Taille, *The Mystery of Faith* (London, 1950), Book II, Thesis XXVI.
13. TCC, p. 915.
14. Ibid., p. 893.

CHAPTER V
1. RIE, vol. II, p. 158.
2. Ibid., vol. III, p. 102.
3. ESR, p. 107.
4. Die Reformation in Deutschland, 2nd edit., vol. I, p. 229.
5. ESR, p. 337.
6. ESR, p. 64.
7. Op. cit., Note 3.
8. ESR, p. 101.
9. ESR, p. 100.
10. Op. cit,. Note 8.
11. *Works*, vol. XV, p. 774.
12. *Against Henry, King of England:* 1522, Works, vol. X, s. II. p. 220.
13. *Courrier de Rome*, No. 74, 10 September, 1970.
14. *Institutes of the Christian Religion*, IV. 18.
15. Works P.S., vol. I, p. 445.
16. CW, vol. I, p. 6.
17. Ibid, p. 238.
18. *Two Epistles of H. Bullynger, with consent of all the learned men of the church*

of Tyrgury (London, 1548 A.v.).

CHAPTER VI
1. CW, vol. I, p. 348.
2. ESR, p. 139.
3. Ibid., p. 142.
4. London, 1956, p. 36.
5. ESR, p. 145.
6. RMP, vol. I, p. 203.
7. EBCP, p. 253.
8. A. G. Dickens, *The English Reformation* (London 1964), p. 270.
9. Op. cit., Note 1.
10. *Letters, Treatises, Remains,* P.S., p. 270.
11. RMP, vol. I, p. 137.
12. CW, vol. I, p. 47.
13. Op. cit., Note 1.
14. *Later Writings,* P.S., p. 32.
15. CW, vol. I, p. 352.
16. Ibid., p. 346.
17. Op. cit., Note 15.
18. Ibid.
19. CDT, vol. III, p. 362.
20. PHR, p. 194.
21. RMP, vol. I, p. 434.
22. VAC, p. 72.
23. CW, vol. I, p. 349.
24. RIE, vol. II, p. 158; RMP, vol. I, p. 380.
25. CDT, vol. III, p. 362.
26. VAC, p. 62.
27. CW, vol. I, p. 350.
28. George Godwin, *The Middle Temple* (London, 1954), p. 69.
29. E. S. Gibson, *The Thirty-Nine Articles of the Church of England* (London, 1898), p. 12.
30. Ibid., p. 84. This very useful book contains the complete text of the Forty-Two Articles.

CHAPTER VII
1. CW, vol. I, p. 52.
2. TR, p. 79.
3. *Early Writings,* P.S., p. 139.

4. EBCP, pp. 129, 131.
5. RMP, vol. I, p. 202.
6. TR, p. 81.
7. A list of them is cited in ESR, p. 162.
8. ESR, p. 112.
9. *Brief Declaration on the Lord's Supper,* P.S., p. 23.
10. ESR, p. 160.
11. ESR, p. 159.
12. PHR, p. 129.
13. Censura, pp. 552-3.
14. Ibid., p. 465. The sacraments are, of course, referred to as sacred signs or symbols within Catholic theology, particularly by St. Augustine. But in Catholic theology the sacraments *effect* what they signify, the baptismal waters do not simply symbolise the removal of original sin, they effect it. (See Appendix I.) The Eucharist is unique, even among the sacraments, for it actually *contains what it signifies,* Christ Himself. ST, III, Q. LXV, art. III.
15. EBCP, p. 275.
16. D, 355. The oath of Berengarius was familiar to Cranmer, see CW, vol. I, pp. 12-14, 196, 203. It is cited in Pope Paul VI's Encyclical Letter *Mysterium Fidei* (C.T.S., London), p. 23.
17. CW, vol. I, p. 57.
18. Ibid., p. 79.
19. Ibid., p. 3.
20. VAC, p. 70.
21. CW, vol. I, p. 203.
22. Ibid., p. 204.
23. VAC, p. 60.
24. RMP, vol. I, p. 429.
25. CW, vol. I, p. 138.
26. Ibid., p. 177.
27. RMP, vol. I, p. 436.
28. Ibid., p. 328.

29. CW, vol. I, p. 229.
30. ESR, p. 555.

CHAPTER VIII
1. RIE, vol. II, p. 158.
2. EBCP, p. 67.
3. RIE, vol. II, p. 83.
4. RMP, vol. I, p. 203.
5. Ibid.
6. RIE, vol. II, p. 109.
7. Ibid., p. 83.
8. FSPB, p. xii.
9. H. Grisar, *Luther* (London, 1913-17), vol. V, p. 145.
10. PHR, p. 114.
11. FSPB, p. 212.
12. RIE, vol. II, p. 109.
13. Ibid.
14. *History of the Doctrine of the Eucharist* (London, 1909), vol. II, p. 139.
15. *The Booke of Common Prayer in the Church of England; its making and revisions, 1549-1561* (London, 1949), p. 15.
16. ESR, p. 194.
17. Ibid., p. 184.
18. RMP, vol. I, p. 414.
19. Ibid., p. 415.
20. ESR, p. 192.
21. RMP, vol. I, p. 266.
22. CW, vol. I, p. 79.
23. RMP, vol. I, p. 380.
24. Ibid.
25. RIE, vol. II, p. 158.
26. ESR, p. 142.
27. RMP, vol. I, p. 293.
28. "The first impression upon a modern Catholic reader made by the reading of these old English Uses will be, we think, one of surprise that he finds himself so much at home in them. They are utterly unlike the 'Communion Service' of the church now established (i.e. Anglican), while we are convinced that if they were re-introduced among us tomorrow our people would scarcely feel any difference." Addis & Arnold's *Catholic Dictionary* (London, 1925), p. 534.
29. In a footnote to the C.T.S. revised 1968 edition Francis Clark comments: "Pope Leo XIII himself explained the nature and scope of the Bull in November 1896, in a letter to Cardinal Richard, Archbishop of Paris. Here he said: 'It was Our intention thereby to deliver a final judgement, and to settle absolutely that most grave question'. He added: 'All Catholics are bound to receive Our decision with the utmost respect, as for ever valid, firm, and irrevocable *(perpetuo firmam, ratam, irrevocabilem)'.*" *Anglican Orders, Final Decision,* C.T.S., p. 22.
30. VAC, p. 54.
31. VAC, p. 42.

CHAPTER IX
1. EBCP, p. 182.
2. Cabrol edition of *The Roman Missal,* introduction.
3. *Pascendi Dominici Gregis,* Burns & Oates, p. 54.
4. RS, p. 70.
5. EBCP, p. 183.
6. ER, p. 119.
7. *The Great Betrayal (Britons, 1970),* p. 8.
8. ST, III, Q. LXXXIII, Art. V.
9. A comprehensive selection of citations from all the principal authorities is given in an article by Fr. Raymond Dulac in the *Courrier de Rome,* Number 15, upon which I have drawn extensively for this chapter.

10. ST, I, IIae, Q. XCVII.
11. *La Nouvelle Messe* (Paris, 1972), p. 40.
12. Pensée, 108, Translation by M. Turnell, *Paschal's Pensées* (London, 1962), p. 140.
13. RS, p. 75.
14. *Reformation aus Rom* (Munich, 1967), p. 42.
15. *De Legibus:* t. 5 and 6.
16. RS, p, 79.
17. RS, p. 86.
18. Cited in *Courrier de Rome*, No. 15.
19. RS, p. 132.
20. VAC, p. 42.
21. RS, p. 59.
22. Part VI, 29.

CHAPTER X
1. TM, p. 208.
2. Ibid., p. 204 and p. 202. See also Note 28 to Chapter VIII.
3. TM, p. 205.
4. Ibid., p. 206.
5. *The Tablet*, 24 July, 1971, p. 724.
6. TM, p. 172.
7. EBCP, p. 197.
8. TM, p. 173.
9. Ibid., p. 183.
10. Ibid., p. 184.
11. Ibid., p. 305.
12. TCC, p. 1056.
13. DCD, Ch. V, Sect. III, I.
14. TM, p. 184. The spread of the Roman rite and the incorporation of Gallican elements is discussed in detail on pp. 172-184 and 199-208.
15. Ibid., p. 225.
16. *Itineraires*, No. 162, p. 40. English translation by Edward Burrows from *The Remnant*, 1 February, 1973.
17. TM, p. 202.
18. Ibid., p. 208.

19. Ibid., p. 211.
20. Ibid., p. 213.
21. Ibid., p. 208 and p. 213.
22. Ibid., p. 213.
23. Introduction to the Cabrol edition of *The Roman Missal* (17th edition). Subsequent quotations from Dom Cabrol come from the same source. As regards the question of the relative antiquity of the different liturgies, the so-called "Anaphora of St. Hippolytus" would date back to the third century if authentic, but its authenticity is still a matter of discussion among scholars.
24. Cited in *A Sharp Critique* (Ogilvie Foundation, 1970), p. 3.
25. Cited in *A Shorter History of the Western Liturgy*, T. Klauser, p. 18.
26. Common of the Dedication of a Church.
27. Dr. J. H. Oswald, cited in *The Holy Sacrifice of the Mass*, N. Gihr (St. Louis, 1908), p. 337.
28. *This is the Mass* (London, 1959), p. 34.
29. Op. cit., Note 27.

CHAPTER XI
1. PHR, p. 30.
2. EBCP, p. 120.
3. Ibid., p. 125.
4. Ibid., p. 118.
5. TE, p. 152.
6. EBCP, pp. 108-9.
7. *Sermons*, P.S., pp. 70-1.
8. EBCP, p. 102.
9. FSPB, Introduction.
10. RMP, vol. I, p. 211 (citing Calvin).
11. RIE, vol. II, p. 113.
12. FSPB, Introduction, p. x.
13. EBCP, p. 58.
14. Ibid., p. 64.

15. Ibid., p. 89.
16. Ibid., p. 102.
17. *The England of Elizabeth: the Structure of Society* (London, 1951), p. 17.
18. FSPB, p. 221.
19. D, 956. The Council of Trent explained that "Since the nature of man is such that without external means he cannot easily be raised to the meditation of divine things, Holy Mother Church has instituted certain rites, namely that some things in the Mass be pronounced in a low tone and others in a louder tone. She has likewise, in accordance with apostolic discipline and tradition, made use of ceremonies such as mystical blessings, lights, incense, vestments, and many other things of this kind whereby both the majesty of so great a sacrifice might be emphasized and the minds of the faithful be excited by those visible signs of religion and piety to the contemplation of those most sublime things which are hidden in this sacrifice." D, 943.
20. EBCP, p. 79.
21. RIE, vol. II, p. 102.
22. TE, p. 153.
23. Original Letters, P.S., pp. 31-2.
24. EBCP, p. 95.
25. FSPB, Introduction, p. vi.
26. Institutes; IV, xviii, 12, col. 1059.
27. *Original Letter*, p. 384.
28. EBCP, p. 256.
29. *Early Writings*, P.S., p. 488.
30. *Original Letters*, P.S. vol. I, p. 79.
31. ESR, p. 188.
32. Ibid., p. 187.

33. RIE, vol. II, pp. 120, 121.
34. CW, vol. II, p. 524.
35. ESR, p. 189.
36. J. G. Ridley, *Nicholas Ridley* (London, 1957), pp. 218-9.
37. CW, vol. II, p. 525.
38. RMP, vol. II, p. 219. Note 1. A rubric in the 1552 Prayer Book directs that the minister shall stand on the north side of the table and no longer face east as in the traditional liturgy. A Protestant author, Dr. Srawley, admits in his book *Liturgy and Worship* that this was to "emphasise the idea of the 'communion feast'." (p. 308).
39. EBCP, p. 98.
40. Ibid., p. 128.

CHAPTER XII
1. VAC, p. 54.
2. FSPB and F. H. Dickinson, *Missale Sarum* (Gregg International Publishers Ltd., 1 Westmead, Farnborough, Hants., England. S.B.N. 576 99711 0).
3. ESR, p. 182, citing T. M. Parker, *The English Reformation to 1558* (Oxford 1950), p. 130.
4. *The English Reformation* (London, 1964), p. 219.
5. TE, p. 154.
6. ESR, p. 183.
7. Ibid.
8. EBCP, p. 224.
9. RMP, vol. I, p. 383. References to Luther's reforms are based upon this chapter (VII) of Fr. Messenger's book.
10. EBCP, p. 220.
11. ESR, 184.
12. EBCP, p. 223.
13. *The Modern Mass*, p. 25.

14. CW, vol. I, p. 79.
15. The Armenian Decree, 1439. D, 715.
16. Works, P.S., p. 26.
17. Works, P.S., 111.
18. RMP, vol. I, p. 387.
19. TM, p. 402.
20. Op. cit., Note 15. D, 698.
21. Op. cit., Note 15.
22. CDT, see entry: *Epiklesis*.
23. RMP, vol. I, p. 388.
24. ESR, p. 186.
25. RMP, vol. I, p. 394.
26. CW, vol. I, p. 139.
27. RMP, vol. I, p. 358.
28. ESR, p. 187.
29. FSPB, p. 230.
30. Ibid., p. 389.
31. Ibid., p. 393.
32. D, 883 and 888.
33. CW, vol. II, p. 432.
34. Op. cit., Chapter VI, Note 29.
35. Ibid., p. 28.
36. Ibid., p. 83.
37. Ibid., p. 645.
38. *The Prayer Book, Articles, and Homilies* (London, 1897), pp. 264-5.
39. Ibid., p. 255.

CHAPTER XIII
1. RMP, vol. I, p. 564.
2. K. Rahner, *The Teaching of the Church* (Cork, 1967), p. 342.
3. Ibid., p. 339.
4. *Agreement on the Doctrine of the Ministry*, Grove Books, Bramcote, Notts, 1973.
5. D, 957.
6. D, 961.
7. D, 958.
8. D, 962.
9. RMP, vol. I, p. 564.
10. TE, p. 162.
11. VAC, p. 78.
12. *The Reformation and the Eucharist* (London, 1927), p. 50.

CHAPTER XIV
1. *The Prayer Book, Articles, and Homilies* (London, 1897), p. 19.
2. TR, p. 118.
3. DEV, p. 233.
4. TUD, p. 50.
5. Op. cit., Note 3.
6. RIE, vol. II, p. 165.
7. Op. cit. Note 3.
8. Ibid., p. 234.
9. TUD, p. 53.
10. Ibid., p. 141.
11. Ibid., p. 57. "The Edwardian Council always regarded the Western Rebellion as primarily religious in purpose. On 11th June, Somerset spoke of an attempt, instigated by 'seditious priests, to seke restitucion of the olde bluddy lawes'. The chroniclers unanimous emphasis on the religious motivation of the rebels is confirmed by their articles, a manifesto for a return to catholicism."
12. Ibid.
13. Ibid., p. 58.
14. Ibid., p. 135.
15. CW, vol. II, pp. 163-187.
16. It is interesting to note that in 1947 Pope Pius XII found it necessary to condemn the proposition that the whole of the eucharistic liturgy is, as Cranmer phrased it, "the act of the people". The essence of the Catholic Mass is that: "The unbloody immolation by which, after the words of consecration have been pronounced, Christ is rendered present on the altar in the state of a victim, is performed by the priest alone, and by the priest in so far as he acts in the name of Christ, not

in so far as he represents the faithful." *Mediator Dei,* C.T.S. edition, para. 96. As was made clear in Chapter XIII, there is all the difference in the world between a priest who possesses powers different not only in degree but in essence from those of the laity, and who offers sacrifice in the person of Christ, and of a minister simply acting as the representative of the faithful by whom he is appointed to preside over their assembly.

17. EBCP, p. 238.
18. Ibid.
19. RIE, vol. II, p. 169.
20. Ibid.
21. Ibid.
22. TE, p. 157.
23. EBCP, p. 254.
24. TUD, p. 55.
25. EBCP, p. 246.

CHAPTER XV
1. TR, p. 122.
2. EBCP, p. 300.
3. Ibid., pp. 257/8.
4. Ibid., p. 300.
5. Ibid., p. 236.
6. Ibid., p. 256.

7. ESR, p. 182.
8. Foxe, *Acts and Monuments,* 8 vols., edit. by J. Pratt (London, 1877), vol. V, p. **527.**
9. Ibid., p. 779.
10. J. T. Tomlinson, *The Prayer Book, Articles, and Homilies* (London, 1897), p. 23.
11. Op. cit., Note 8, p. 763.
12. Ibid., p. 784.
13. EBCP, p. 245.
14. ESR, p. 187.
15. TE, p. 161.
16. *Original Letters,* p. 72.
17. EBCP, p. 271.
18. TE, p. 168.
19. DEV, pp. 235-6.
20. RIE, vol. II, p. 126.
21. TR, p. 120.
22. TE, p. 164.

CHAPTER XVI
1. EBCP, p. 81.
2. RMP, vol. I, p. 414.
3. Quoted in *The Tablet,* Nov. 28, 1925.
4. TE, p. 164.
5. RIE, vol. III, p. 38.
6. TR, p. 132.
7. RIE, vol. III, pp. 89-90.
8. TR, p. 285.
9. Op. cit., Chapter X, Note 17.

INDEX